ISSUES THAT CONCERN YOU

Drug Abuse

Arthur Gillard, *Book Editor*

W9-BHG-466

GREENHAVEN PRESS
A part of Gale, Cengage Learning

GALE
CENGAGE Learning·

Detroit • New York • San Francisco • New Haven, Conn • Waterville, Maine • London

CONTENTS

Drug abuse exacts a terrible toll on society. In financial terms alone the cost is enormous. The National Center on Addiction and Substance Abuse at Columbia University (CASA) estimates total costs at federal, state, and local levels as a result of drug abuse to be $467.7 billion each year. And as addiction recovery expert John Dupuy points out, "Although the dollar amounts are staggering, it hardly touches on the emotional and spiritual costs of [drug abuse and] addiction—the lost and wasted human potential, the devastation to families and communities."[1] Drug abuse contributes to child abuse and neglect, crime, accidents, homelessness, premature death, and debilitating disease.

It's important to distinguish between drug use, drug abuse, and addiction. Drug use simply means deliberate ingestion of a drug to alter consciousness. Drug abuse might be defined as a pattern of drug use that creates significant harm for the user or others. Addiction is a condition of strong dependence on a drug, such that it becomes almost impossible for the addicted person to resist taking the drug, no matter how devastating the consequences may be. Addiction is one of the more serious consequences of drug abuse, and although some are more susceptible than others, it can happen to anyone. As David Nutt, chair of the Independent Scientific Committee on Drugs and the author of *Drugs Without the Hot Air: Minimising the Harms of Legal and Illegal Drugs*, explains, "We now understand that repeated use of a drug can cause physical changes to our brains, resulting in a kind of 'brain disease,' in the same way that strain on the heart can lead to heart disease. Neuroimaging techniques in the last 15 years have allowed us to see these changes for the first time, confirming that these changes are physical and to an extent irreversible."[2]

Teenagers may be particularly at risk. David Walsh, author of *Why Do They Act That Way? A Survival Guide to the Adolescent Brain for You and Your Teen*, explains, "Brain science reveals how alcohol and other drugs affect the adolescent brain differently than the adult brain: the young brain is more easily addicted. Damage done to the brain can be more severe on a dose for dose basis. Teens tend to underestimate risk and ignore warning signals leading to more treacherous consequences."[3] Echoing that last point, A. Thomas McLellan notes that "the major worry of teen substance use is not addiction; it is overdose, accidents, contraction of diseases, etc. It is harder to anticipate these kinds of risks."[4]

Everyone concerned with issues of drug abuse wants to improve the situation, but there is much disagreement over what is to be done. Some argue for total abstinence from or prohibition of drugs, although those who hold such positions often exempt some mind-altering substances—usually alcohol, tobacco, or caffeine—from what they consider to be "drugs." Others would prefer a medical approach; for example, substituting the synthetic narcotic methadone for heroin to treat heroin addiction, or giving alcoholics the drug Antabuse, which makes alcohol consumption feel unpleasant and therefore unrewarding. Another proposed solution is to encourage people to use drugs in healthier ways, such as encouraging moderate alcohol consumption rather than binge-drinking.

Advances in science and technology promise additional possibilities in the decades to come, both intriguing and unsettling in their implications. Some scientists are hard at work trying to develop vaccines that will neutralize drugs as soon as they enter the bloodstream, preventing them from having an effect. Nutt explains the dilemmas this may give rise to:

> Vaccines for nicotine and cocaine are currently under clinical development, with a view to helping addicted users stop their habits. If this works then the question arises whether we could or should vaccinate people to protect them from developing an addiction in the first place, just as we do today with vaccines for polio and whooping cough. Even more controversial is the question of whether vaccines like this should be administered to children to immunize them against drug and alcohol use. Is it violating somebody's human rights to take away their choice to experience pleasure from a drug at some point in the future?[5]

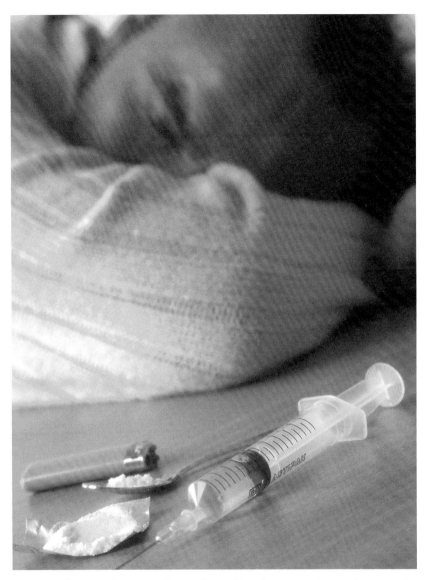

In just financial costs, drug abuse has been estimated to total $467.7 billion at the federal, state, and local levels.

Another active area of research involves using psychedelic drugs such as ibogaine and psilocybin, which are not themselves addictive but appear to be useful in treating addictions to drugs such as nicotine, alcohol, and heroin. More speculatively, some suggest that safer recreational drugs might be developed. For example, early research has shown promise in blocking some of the harmful effects of alcohol, suggesting that it might be possible to create alcoholic drinks that produce the pleasant effects without some of the harmful side effects.

Perhaps, for now at least, prevention through education is the best approach. According to Winifred Rosen and Andrew T. Weil, authors of *From Chocolate to Morphine: Everything You Need to Know About Mind-Altering Drugs*, "Preventing drug abuse is a realistic goal. Two approaches are possible. One is to teach people, especially young people, how to satisfy their needs and desires without recourse to drugs. The second is to teach people how to form good relationships with drugs so that if they choose to use drugs, they will continue to be users and never become abusers." As they note, "Any drug can be used successfully, no matter how bad its reputation, and any drug can be abused, no matter how accepted it is. There are no good or bad drugs; there are only good and bad relationships with drugs."[6]

In exploring this topic, keep in mind that although there is an increasing amount of useful information on the subject of drug abuse, with so much controversy surrounding the issue, there is also bound to be much that is misleading as well. As Nutt points out, "Unfortunately, there's an awful lot of misinformation about drugs, both on the Internet and in the media. Any source that says 'all drugs are evil' or 'taking drugs is totally fine' is definitely not to be trusted!"[7]

Authors in this anthology offer a variety of perspectives on drug abuse. In addition, the volume contains a thorough bibliography, a list of organizations to contact for further information, and appendices to help the reader understand and explore the topic. The appendix titled "What You Should Know About Drug Abuse" offers facts about the problem that can be used in writing papers or for debates. The appendix "What You Should Do About Drug Abuse" offers advice for young people who are concerned with this issue. With all these features, *Issues That Concern You: Drug Abuse* provides an excellent resource for everyone interested in this persistent topic.

Notes

1. John Dupuy, *Integral Recovery: A Revolutionary Approach to the Treatment of Alcoholism and Addiction*. New York: State University of New York Press, 2013, pp. 3–4.
2. David Nutt, *Drugs Without the Hot Air: Minimising the Harms of Legal and Illegal Drugs*. Cambridge: UIT Cambridge Ltd., 2012, p. 133.
3. CASA (The National Center on Addiction and Substance Abuse at Columbia University), *Adolescent Substance Use: America's #1 Public Health Problem*, June 2011, p. 12. www .casacolumbia.org/upload/2011/20110629adolescentsubstance use.pdf.
4. CASA, *Adolescent Substance Use*, p. 51.
5. Nutt, *Drugs Without the Hot Air*, p. 299.
6. Winifred Rosen and Andrew T. Weil, *From Chocolate to Morphine: Everything You Need to Know About Mind-Altering Drugs*. New York: Mariner, 2004, pp. 3, 29.
7. Nutt, *Drugs Without the Hot Air*, p. 312.

ONE

An Overview of Drug Abuse and Dependence

Genevieve Pham-Kanter and Teresa G. Odle

Genevieve Pham-Kanter is an assistant professor in the School of Public Health and the Department of Economics at the University of Colorado–Denver. Teresa G. Odle is a writer and editor who has worked in health care communication for many years and is a member of the American Medical Writers Association. In the following viewpoint the authors describe the nature of drug abuse and dependence (using the alternate terms "substance abuse/dependence"). According to the authors, the highest rates of substance abuse and dependence occur in those aged eighteen to twenty-five and are twice as likely to be found in men as in women. Problems such as teen pregnancy, assault, rape, homelessness, and robbery are associated with drug abuse, and estimates of the cost to society range from tens of billions to hundreds of billions of dollars. The authors say that overdose is a particular risk of substance abuse, which may be due to carelessness on the part of the user, unpredictable potency of drugs purchased from street dealers, or other factors.

Genevieve Pham-Kanter and Teresa G. Odle, "Substance Abuse and Dependence," *The Gale Encyclopedia of Children's Health: Infancy Through Adolescence*, ed. Jacqueline L. Longe, vol. 4, Second Edition. Detroit: Gale, 2011, pp. 2116–2122. The Gale Encyclopedia of Children's Health: Infancy Through Adolescence, 1E. Copyright © 2006 Cengage Learning.

Substance abuse and dependence refer to any continued pathological use of a medication, non-medically indicated drug . . . , or toxin. They normally are distinguished as follows.

Substance abuse is any pattern of substance use that results in repeated adverse social consequences related to drug-taking—for example, interpersonal conflicts; failure to meet work, family, or school obligations; or legal problems. Substance dependence, commonly known as addiction, is characterized by the physiological and behavioral symptoms related to substance use. These symptoms include the need for increasing amounts of the substance to maintain desired effects, withdrawal if drug-taking ceases, and a great deal of time spent in activities related to substance use.

Substance abuse is more likely to be diagnosed among those who have just begun taking drugs and is often an early symptom of substance dependence. However, substance dependence can appear without substance abuse, and substance abuse can persist for extended periods of time without a transition to substance dependence.

Consequences of Drug Abuse and Dependence

Substance abuse and dependence are disorders that affect all population groups although specific patterns of abuse and dependence vary with age, gender, culture, and socioeconomic status. . . .

Although substance dependence can begin at any age, people aged 18 to 25 have been found to have higher substance abuse and dependency rates than other age groups. Individuals who first used drugs or alcohol at a young age are more likely to have drug abuse and dependence problems later in life than those who first used drugs or alcohol at an older age. Gender proportions vary according to the class of drugs, but substance abuse and dependence is about twice as likely to occur in men than in women.

In addition to being an individual health disorder, substance abuse and dependence may be viewed as a public health problem with far-ranging health, economic, and social implications. Substance-related disorders are associated with teen pregnancy and the transmission of sexually transmitted diseases (STDs), as well as failure in school, unemployment, domestic violence, homelessness, and crimes such as rape and sexual assault, aggravated assault, robbery, burglary, and larceny. Many different estimates have been made for the economic cost of substance abuse and dependence, and most estimate it at tens or hundreds of billions of dollars. . . .

Types of Abused Substances

Substances have an intoxicating effect, desired by the user, which can have either stimulating (speeding up) or depressive/sedating (slowing down) effects on the body. Substance dependence and/or abuse can involve any of the following 10 classes of substances:

- alcohol
- amphetamines (including "crystal meth," some medications used in the treatment of attention deficit disorder [ADD], and amphetamine-like substances found in appetite suppressants)
- cannabis (including marijuana and hashish)
- cocaine (including "crack")
- hallucinogens (including LSD, mescaline, and MDMA [ecstasy])
- inhalants (including compounds found in gasoline, glue, and paint thinners)
- nicotine (including that found in cigarettes and smokeless tobacco)
- opioids (including morphine, heroin, codeine, methadone, oxycodone [OxyContin])
- phencyclidine (including PCP, angel dust, ketamine)
- sedative, hypnotic, and anxiolytic (anti-anxiety) substances (including benzodiazepines such as valium, barbiturates, prescription sleeping medications, and most prescription anti-anxiety medications)

Caffeine has been identified as a substance in this context, but as yet there is insufficient evidence to establish whether caffeine-related symptoms fall under substance abuse and dependence.

Individuals who use drugs or alcohol at an early age are more likely to have drug abuse and dependency problems later in life than those who wait until adulthood or who never use drugs at all.

Substances of abuse may thus be illicit drugs, readily available substances such as alcohol or glue, over-the-counter drugs, or prescription medications. In many cases, a prescription medication that becomes a substance of abuse may have been a legal, medically indicated prescription for the user, but the pattern of use diverges from the use prescribed by the physician.

Causes of Substance-Related Disorders

The causes of substance dependence are not well established, but three factors are believed to contribute to substance-related disorders: genetic factors, psychopathology, and social learning. In genetic epidemiological studies of alcoholism, the probability of identical twins both exhibiting alcohol dependence was significantly greater than with fraternal twins, thus suggesting a genetic component in alcoholism. It is unclear, however, whether the genetic factor is related to alcoholism directly, or whether it is linked to other psychiatric disorders that are known to be associated with substance abuse. For example, there is evidence that alcoholic males from families with depressive disorders tend to have more severe courses of substance dependence than alcoholic men from families without such histories.

These and other findings suggest substance use may be [a] way to relieve the symptoms of a psychological disorder. In this model, unless the underlying pathology is treated, attempts to permanently stop substance dependence are ineffective. Psychopathologies that are associated with substance dependence include antisocial personality disorder, bipolar disorder, depression, anxiety disorder, and schizophrenia.

A third factor related to substance dependence is social environment. In this model, drug-taking is essentially a socially learned behavior. . . . For example, individuals may, by observing family or peer role models, learn that substance use is a normal way to relieve daily stresses. External penalties, such as legal or social sanctions, may reduce the likelihood of substance use. . . .

Symptoms of Substance Dependence/Addiction

The DSM-IV-TR [*Diagnostic and Statistical Manual of Mental Disorders*, revised 4th edition, the reference book used by mental health professionals to diagnose mental illness] identifies seven criteria (symptoms), at least three of which must be met during a given 12-month period, for the diagnosis of substance dependence:

- Tolerance, as defined either by the need for increasing amounts of the substance to obtain the desired effect or by experiencing less effect with extended use of the same amount of the substance.

- Withdrawal, as exhibited either by experiencing unpleasant mental, physiological, and emotional changes when drug-taking ceases or by using the substance as a way to relieve or prevent withdrawal symptoms.
- Longer duration of taking substance or use in greater quantities than was originally intended.
- Persistent desire or repeated unsuccessful efforts to stop or lessen substance use.
- A relatively large amount of time spent in securing and using the substance, or in recovering from the effects of the substance.
- Important work and social activities reduced because of substance use.
- Continued substance use despite negative physical and psychological effects of use.

Although not explicitly listed in the DSM-IV-TR criteria, "craving," or the overwhelming desire to use the substance regardless of countervailing forces, is a universally reported symptom of substance dependence. . . .

Overdosing on a substance is a frequent complication of substance abuse. Drug overdose can be purposeful (with suicide as a goal), or due to carelessness, the unpredictable strength of substances purchased from street dealers, the mixing of more than one type of substance, or as a result of the increasing doses that a person must take to experience a similar level of effect. Substance overdose can be a life-threatening emergency, with the specific symptoms depending on the type of substance used. Substances with depressive effects may dangerously slow the breathing and heart rate, drop the body temperature, and result in general unresponsiveness. Substances with stimulatory effects may dangerously increase the heart rate and blood pressure, produce abnormal heart rhythms, increase body temperature, induce seizures, and cause erratic behavior. . . .

Treating Substance Use Disorders

According to the American Psychiatric Association, there are three goals for the treatment of people with substance use disorders: (1) the patient abstains from or reduces the use and effects of the substance; (2) the patient reduces the frequency and severity of relapses; and (3) the patient develops the psychological and emotional skills necessary to restore and maintain personal, occupational, and social functioning.

In general, before treatment can begin, many treatment centers require that the patient undergo detoxification. Detoxification is the process of weaning the patient from his or her regular substance use. Detoxification can be accomplished "cold turkey," by complete and immediate cessation of all substance use, or by slowly decreasing (tapering) the dose the individual is taking, to minimize the side effects of withdrawal. Some substances must be tapered because "cold turkey" methods of detoxification are potentially life threatening. In some cases, medications may be used to combat the physical and psychological symptoms of withdrawal. For example, methadone is used to help patients adjust to the tapering off of heroin use. . . .

Recovery from substance use is notoriously difficult, even with exceptional treatment resources. Although relapse rates are difficult to accurately obtain, the NIAAA [National Institute on Alcohol Abuse and Alcoholism] cites evidence that 90% of alcohol dependent users experience at least one relapse within the 4 years after treatment. Relapse rates for heroin and nicotine users are believed to be similar. Certain pharmacological treatments, however, have been shown to reduce relapse rates.

Relapses are most likely to occur within the first 12 months of having discontinued substance use. Triggers for relapses can include any number of life stresses . . . , in addition to seemingly mundane exposure to a place, situation, or acquaintance associated with previous substance use.

The development of adaptive life skills and ongoing drug-free social support are believed to be two important factors in avoiding relapse. . . . Support for family members in addition to support for the individual in recovery is also important. Because substance

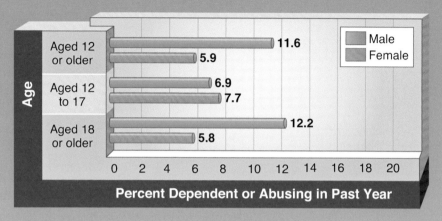

Substance Dependence or Abuse in the Past Year, by Age and Gender, 2010

Age		
Aged 12 or older	Male: 11.6	Female: 5.9
Aged 12 to 17	Male: 6.9	Female: 7.7
Aged 18 or older	Male: 12.2	Female: 5.8

Percent Dependent or Abusing in Past Year

Taken from: Fig. 7.6 (Substance Dependence or Abuse in the Past Year, by Age and Gender: 2010). Substance Abuse and Mental Health Services Administration (SAMHSA), results from the 2010 National Survey on Drug Use and Health: Summary of National Findings, September 2011. www.samhsa.gov/data/NSDUH/2k10NSDUH/2k10Results.htm.

dependence has a serious impact on family functioning, and because family members may inadvertently maintain behaviors that initially led to the substance dependence, ongoing therapy and support for family members should not be neglected.

Prevention Through Education and Training

Prevention is best aimed at teenagers and young adults aged 18–24 who are at very high risk for substance experimentation. Prevention programs should include an education component that outlines the risks and consequences of substance use and a training component that gives advice on how to resist peer pressure to use drugs.

Furthermore, prevention programs should work to identify and target children who are at relatively higher risk for substance abuse. This group includes victims of physical or sexual abuse, children of parents who have a history of substance abuse, and children with poor school performance and/or attention deficit disorder. These children may require more intensive intervention.

TWO

Drug Abusers Are Often Victims of a Mental Illness

Harold Koplewicz

> Harold Koplewicz is a child and adolescent psychiatrist and the president of the Child Mind Institute. In the following viewpoint Koplewicz argues that drug addiction is a mental illness that is not the fault of the drug abuser. He asserts that as with persons with other mental illnesses, such as depression or schizophrenia, people ought to approach addicts with nonjudgmental compassion. He acknowledges that in areas where drug abuse is rampant, law enforcement efforts are appropriate, but he claims that the underlying problems that lead to drug abuse and addiction require a deeper response. He contends that what is needed to avert the high human and financial cost of addiction is early intervention and a holistic approach that addresses dysfunction in the addict, her or his family, and the community at large.

I like to think that we are making great progress in the fight against the stigma of mental illness—a fight that is necessary to ensure that people of any age with psychiatric or learning disorders feel comfortable getting the care they need. Once-taboo issues like depression, bipolar disorder, PTSD [post-traumatic stress disorder] and dyslexia are now out in the open, and everyone from pop stars and movie stars, to soldiers and professional athletes, are comfortable admitting their problems and seeking help. We've come a long way.

But we still have a long way to go. Even those who are kind, caring and non-judgmental when it comes to most psychiatric disorders, from selective mutism to schizophrenia, may change their tune when talk turns to drug abuse and addiction. "Drunks," "junkies," "stoners"—we look down on them because they "chose" to become addicted to drugs. They "chose" to ruin families and relationships. They made a "choice" that cost them their lives in an overdose.

Addiction Is a No-Fault Mental Illness

This "choice" is a false one. Drug abuse and addiction are tragic things, but they are not character traits. Just as depression is a no-fault mental illness, so is addiction. And just as depression can tragically lead to suicide, so addiction can lead to self-inflicted death by overdose. They are both mistakes—profound mistakes— that the illness makes people more likely to make. But we can, should and must help suffering young people avoid them. This means tackling addiction, which takes the lives of people every year. But how?

A recent [2011] *New York Times* article tells the sobering story of an Ohio county in the grip of a prescription drug abuse epidemic that has taken the lives of many young people. In the article, Sabrina Tavernise lays out some devastating statistics: In Scioto County, almost 1 in 10 babies test positive for drugs at birth. In Ohio as a whole, overdoses have long since outpaced car accidents as a cause of death. Prescription drug addiction across the nation is "now killing more people than crack cocaine in the 1980s and heroin in the 1970s combined."

I don't have to say that the drugs abused tend not to be medications for diabetes or high blood pressure, depression or schizophrenia. They tend to be habit-forming pain medications, like the OxyContin that has claimed dozens of lives in the town of Portsmouth, Ohio.

The suggestion is that the declining economy—locally and nationally—has brought on this tragedy, and urban decay and loss of industry are certainly at play. But the article fails to recognize that the root of much prescription drug misuse is untreated mental illness, which not only can lead to drug abuse but can also

Just like depression, drug addiction can lead to suicide from drug overdose.

be exacerbated by environmental factors, like poverty. Anxiety and depression can come unbidden, but can also be triggered by adverse experiences.

Early Intervention and Treatment Needed

It's the same way with addiction, which is just as much a problem of the mind. Self-medicating with prescription painkillers in stressful situations—what we call a maladaptive coping mechanism—starts many drug abusers on the road to serious problems. In the community Sabrina Tavernise writes about, the abuse is so ubiquitous it is surely a law enforcement issue. But behind the law enforcement issue and tangled with the economic issue is a mental health issue. Tavernise notes that Ohio's governor has pledged $36 million to address the drug problem through prevention and rehabilitation, which I applaud, but what constitutes prevention? Locals want more direct police intervention, shutting down clinics that (perhaps unlawfully) dispense pain medication and the like. But the problem is more deeply ingrained in the people, nuanced and immune to the number of cops on the street.

"We're raising third and fourth generations of prescription drug abusers now," the Portsmouth police chief tells Tavernise. These problems are deeply rooted in families—just as some other psychiatric disorders can be—and the only way to reliably prevent them is to both intervene early with kids and treat the whole family in order to mitigate the influence of a potentially corrupting disease. The goal is to make the family what it should be—a nurturing, positive force.

Not everyone who commits suicide is mentally ill, but mental illnesses, like depression and bipolar disorder, make people feel hopeless and therefore much more likely to commit suicide. Likewise, not everyone who overdoses is addicted, but addiction greatly increases the likelihood of overdose. The bottom line is that addiction is an illness that we are able to treat and manage, if not cure, provided that we focus on the person with the addiction, the family and the community—a holistic approach to a sprawling problem.

Substance Dependence or Abuse in the Past Year and Mental Illness Among Adults Aged 18 or Older, 2010

Almost half of people suffering from SUD (substance use disorder, e.g., substance abuse or substance addiction) also suffer from mental illness.

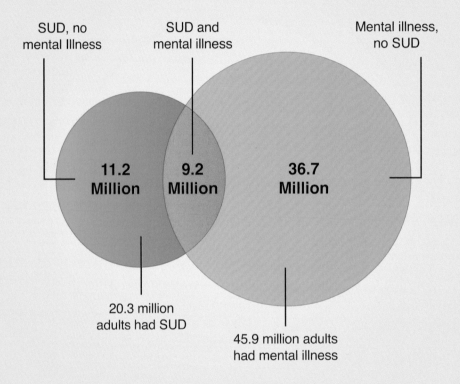

SUD, no mental Illness

SUD and mental illness

Mental illness, no SUD

11.2 Million

9.2 Million

36.7 Million

20.3 million adults had SUD

45.9 million adults had mental illness

Taken from: Figure. 4.2. "Results from the 2010 National Survey on Drug Use and Health: Mental Health Findings." Substance Abuse and Mental Health Services Administration (SAMHSA), January 2012. www.samhsa.gov/data/nsduh/2k10MH_Findings/2k10MHResults.htm.

"I miss her so much," says the mother of an addict who was murdered by a home invader looking for pills. "If you had 100 kids, you'll never replace the one you've lost."

For this mother, I think the crime might as well have been an overdose or suicide. Her child is gone because of addiction. Let's help make sure no more children are lost to this disease.

THREE

People Are Responsible for Their Decision to Abuse Drugs

Ashley Hames

> Ashley Hames is a British writer and the author of the book *Adventures of a Sex Reporter*. In the following viewpoint Hames claims that addiction is not a "disease" that compels people to use drugs. Rather, he argues that drug use is a personal choice that people make, which often has very negative consequences. The author uses himself as an example and says that he made a series of personal decisions to use cocaine and sleeping pills. According to Hames, addiction should be seen as a long-term physical consequence of chosen drug use, rather than as a disease, and he notes that while people can avoid using drugs, they cannot choose to avoid having a true disease such as Parkinson's disease. Hames says that considering addiction a disease over which people have no control is a way of avoiding responsibility for the consequences of drug use; e.g., the deaths of people involved in the drug trade.

Words are important. Labels are important. And it's my view that labelling drug addiction as a 'disease' is dangerous and wrong.

No-one I have known in my immediate family has, to the best of my knowledge, suffered from any serious addiction. These, however, are the boxes I can tick: alcohol, drugs, sex, gambling.

As far as drugs are concerned, cocaine and sleeping pills were my drugs of choice. And yes, it was a choice. I chose them. They did not choose me. It wasn't like I woke up one day and discovered I had this terrible 'disease' which wasn't my fault and for which I should receive your sympathy and compassion.

I agree that drug *addiction* should be dealt with by doctors and not by policemen. But we shouldn't make the mistake of labelling that addiction as a disease. Addiction is an illness caused by taking too many drugs for too long, the physical reaction to excessive use. I don't mean to be unsympathetic—I feel desperately sorry for the many vulnerable people who made the leap into drugs and slipped too far. All I'm saying here is that to call drug abuse a 'disease' is wrong.

Personal Responsibility

This is more than just semantics. By labelling drug abusers as 'diseased,' we negate them from any real sense of responsibility for their individual actions. I'm all for a bit of love and compassion, but let's get real here and call things by their proper names. Taking drugs is avoidable, Parkinson's [disease] is not.

I can't stress this enough, but when you initially take drugs you are essentially making a life gamble: Can I handle this or not? If you can't, then you'll lose the bet and become an addict.

You may lose everything, including your life. If you're lucky—and many of us are—you won't. But the decision to take drugs is not ingrained in your DNA, it's not a genetic fault-line, it's just . . . a gamble. By calling it a 'disease' we're implying that in a drug-free parallel universe you'd still fall 'ill,' succumb to your 'disease' and start seeking out substances that you didn't even know existed.

Taking drugs is a decision, not a disease.

Reasons for Using Drugs

People use narcotics usually for one of two things—for the pursuit of pleasure, or to escape painful memories. And drugs can, initially, be great fun, and they can also be a vacuous obliteration. And then addiction can take over, at which point, sure, a

The Relative Harm to Users and Others Caused by Various Drugs

Drugs cause harm both to the individuals using them and to society at large. Harms to the individual include impairment of mental functioning, loss of relationships, injury, and damage to physical health. Harms to others include increase in crime (e.g., to get money for drugs), environmental harm caused by drug production, increase in international crime (such as drug-trafficking-related violence), family breakdown, and increased financial costs (e.g., for health care and imprisonment). The following chart, created by the Independent Scientific Committee on Drugs (ISCD), attempts to define the relative harmfulness of various drugs—both legal and illegal—to the user and others. The score of each drug (e.g., 55 for heroin) is arrived at by combining ratings of various types of harm using a technique called multicriteria decision analysis (MCDA).

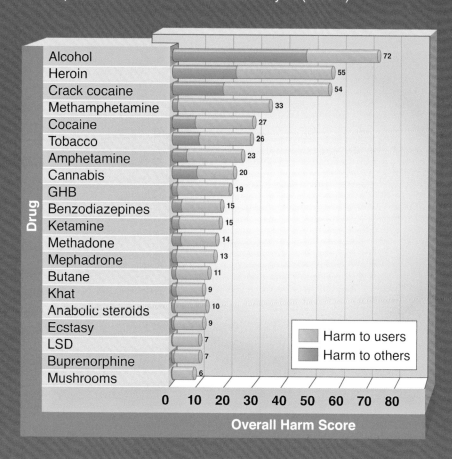

Taken from: "Drug Harms in the UK: A Multicriteria Decision Analysis." David J Nutt, Leslie A. King, Lawrence D. Phillips, on behalf of the Independent Scientific Committee on Drugs. *Lancet* 2010; 376: 1558–1565 published online November 1, 2010. www.fcaglp.unlp.edu.ar/~mmiller/espanol/Variedades,%20politica/drogas_Journal.pdf.

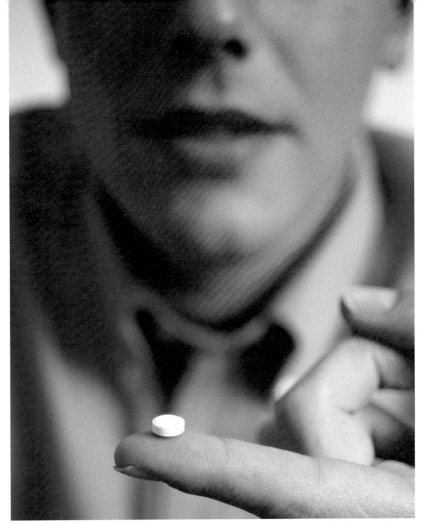

The author argues that labeling drug abusers as "diseased" relieves them from any sense of responsibility for their choice to use drugs.

medical condition results. But it's a choice first, and a condition later; let's not label the telephone call to your dealer a symptom of some greater 'disease.'

To think of my drug-taking activities as a medical condition is a complete cop-out. Did this disease make me roll up that ten pound note, stick it up my nose and snort a line of cocaine? Hardly. It was impulsive behaviour and impulsive behaviour is exactly that—behaviour.

In life, we define ourselves by what we do, and if we choose drugs, the choice is ours, not some indefinable, ethereal illness.

There's no disease controlling me if I decide to chop out a line. For me, it was usually just a temporary error of judgement and an appetite for self-destruction. For others it may be something different, but whatever it is, it's got nothing to do with disease.

Someone like [British comedian and actor] Russell Brand . . . has received the best therapy money can buy, treatment which has succeeded, I believe, only in brainwashing him into thinking he's devoid of all responsibility for his actions. For someone so self-indulgent, that's the best medical diagnosis he could possibly have heard. No wonder he's embraced it so warmly. . . .

The Consequences of Drug Use

Brand said that "the illegality makes no difference, the consequences in the country of origin makes no difference."

With the comforting blanket of having been told he has an illness, people like Russell can sleep soundly at night, for in his diseased heart he knows it was never his fault that blood was spilled in the poppy fields of Afghanistan to feed his former addiction. Perhaps a poverty-stricken drug mule died from ingesting a stash of the brown stuff destined for his front door. Well, don't look at Russell, it was beyond his control. Another contract killing in the slums of Rio? Nothing to do with Russell; please don't disturb him, he's dozing.

As long as the use of drugs is considered a disease then we are all blameless, we can all carry on obeying the higher calling of our 'illness' and stick another needle in our arm and to hell with the consequences. Leave us alone, we're stricken.

I'm not saying you should or shouldn't take drugs, but if we do then we should face the consequences of that drug use, deal with the guilt and shame, accept responsibility and know that you, that I, and that thousands of others have caused misery, both on our own doorstep and many miles away, to countless faceless, impoverished individuals. . . .

Brand said "I think that there's a degree of cowardice and wilful ignorance around this condition. . . ."

I couldn't agree more.

FOUR

Social and Environmental Conditions Cause Drug Addiction

Gabor Maté

Gabor Maté is a physician in Vancouver, British Columbia, Canada, and author of *In the Realm of Hungry Ghosts: Close Encounters with Addiction*. In the following viewpoint Maté argues that environmental factors affecting brain development in infants and young children predispose those people to vulnerability to drug abuse and addiction. He points out that most brain development occurs after birth and says current research shows that when animals—including humans—are exposed to certain kinds of stress when they are young, their brains will be deficient in ways that make drugs of abuse more rewarding. According to the author, addicts invariably feel alone and have never experienced unconditional love from parental figures. He cites a series of studies done on "adverse childhood experiences" by the US Centers for Disease Control and Prevention, which found that stressful experiences in childhood such as addiction in other family members, abuse, or a difficult divorce lead to addiction later in life.

Gabor Maté, "Why Punish Pain," *Yes! Magazine*, June 10, 2011. Gabor Maté adapted this article from *Beyond Prisons*, the Summer 2011 issue of YES! Magazine, from his book, *In The Realm of Hungry Ghosts: Close Encounters with Addiction*.

The early 19th-century literary figure Thomas de Quincey was an opium user. "The subtle powers lodged in this mighty drug," he enthused, "tranquilize all irritations of the nervous system . . . stimulate the capacities of enjoyment . . . sustain through twenty-four hours the else drooping animal energies . . . O just, subtle and all-conquering opium . . . Thou only givest these gifts to man; and thou hast the keys of Paradise." A patient of mine in Vancouver's infamous Downtown Eastside said it more plainly: "The reason I do drugs is so that I don't feel the f***ing feelings I feel when I don't do drugs."

All drug addicts, even (or perhaps especially) the abject and marginalized street user, seek in their habit the same paradise de Quincey rhapsodized: a sense of comfort, vitality, and freedom from pain. It's a doomed search that puts in peril their health, societal position, dignity, and freedom. "I'm not afraid of death," another patient told me. "I'm more afraid of life." What kind of despair could lead someone to value short-term pain relief over life itself? And what might be the source of such despair?

Causal Assumptions Ignore Societal Responsibility

In North America, two assumptions inform social attitudes toward addiction. First is the notion that addiction is a result of individual choice, of personal failure, a view that underlies the legal approach toward substance dependence. If the behavior is a matter of choice, then it makes sense to punish or deter it by means of legal sanctions, including incarceration for mere possession. The second perspective is the medical model that sees addiction as an inherited disease of the brain. This view at least has the virtue of not blaming the afflicted person—after all, people cannot help what genes they inherit—and it also offers the possibility of compassionate treatment. . . .

What the choice and heredity hypotheses share in common is that they take society off the hook. Neither compels us to consider how a person's experience and social position contribute to a predisposition for addiction. If oppressed or marginalized populations suffer a disproportionate share of addiction's burden—

Nineteenth-century author Thomas de Quincey, an opium user, believed that drugs give one a sense of comfort, vitality, and freedom from psychological and physical pain.

as they do, here and elsewhere—it must be due to their faulty decision-making or to their flawed genes. The heredity and choice-based models also spare us, conveniently, from looking at how our social environment supports, or does not support, the parents of young children, and at how social attitudes and policies burden, stress, and exclude certain segments of the population and thereby increase their propensity for addiction.

Another, starker view emerges when we listen to the life histories of substance abusers and look at the ample research data.

Addictions always originate in unhappiness, even if hidden. They are emotional anesthetics; they numb pain. The first question—always—is not "Why the addiction?" but "Why the pain?" The answer was summed up with crude eloquence, scrawled on the wall of my patient Anna's room: "Any place I went to, I wasn't wanted. And that bites large."

The Influence of Life Experience

For 12 years I was staff physician at the Portland Hotel, a nonprofit, harm-reduction facility in the Downtown Eastside, an area with an addict population of 3,000 to 5,000. Most of the Portland's clients are addicted to cocaine, crystal meth, alcohol, opiates like heroin, or tranquilizers—or to any combination of these things.

"The first time I did heroin," one of my patients, a 27-year-old sex-trade worker, once told me, "it felt like a warm, soft hug." In a phrase, she summed up the deep psychological and chemical cravings that make some people vulnerable to substance dependence.

Contrary to popular myth, no drug is inherently addictive. Only a small percentage of people who try alcohol or cocaine or even crystal meth go on to addictive use. What makes those people vulnerable? According to current brain research and developmental psychology, chemical and emotional vulnerability are the products not of genetic programming but of life experience. Most of the human brain's growth occurs after birth, and so physical and emotional interactions determine much of our neurological development—which brain areas will develop and how well, which patterns will be encoded, and so on. As such, each brain's circuitry and chemistry reflect individual life experiences as much as inherited tendencies.

Drugs affect the brain by binding to receptors on nerve cells. Opiates work on our built-in receptors for endorphins—the body's own, natural opiate-like substances that participate in many functions, including regulation of pain and mood. Similarly, tranquilizers of the benzodiazepine class, such as Valium, exert their effect at the brain's natural benzodiazepine receptors. Other brain chemicals, including dopamine and serotonin, affect such diverse functions as mood, incentive- and reward-seeking behavior, and self-regulation. These, too, bind to specific, specialized receptors on neurons.

But the number of receptors and level of brain chemicals are not set at birth. Infant rats who get less grooming from their mothers end up with fewer natural "benzo" receptors in the part of the brain that controls anxiety. Brains of infant monkeys separated from their mothers for only a few days are measurably deficient in dopamine.

It is the same with human beings. Endorphins are released in the infant's brain when there are warm, non-stressed, calm interactions with the parenting figures. Endorphins, in turn, promote the growth of receptors and nerve cells, and the discharge of other important brain chemicals. The fewer endorphin-enhancing experiences in infancy and early childhood, the greater the need for external sources. Hence, a greater vulnerability to addictions.

Chronicles of Pain

What sets skid row addicts apart is the extreme degree of stress they had to endure early in life. Almost all women now inhabiting "Canada's addiction capital"—as the Downtown Eastside of Vancouver has been called—suffered sexual assaults in childhood, as did many of the males. Childhood memories of serial abandonment or severe physical and psychological abuse are common. My patients' histories are chronicles of pain upon pain.

Feeling alone, the sense that there has never been anyone with whom to share their deepest emotions, is universal among drug addicts.

Carl, a 36-year-old Native [American] man, was banished from one foster home after another, had dishwashing liquid poured down his throat for using foul language at age 5, and was tied to a chair in a dark room to control his hyperactivity. When angry at himself he gouges his foot with a knife as punishment.

But what of families where there was not abuse, but love; where parents did their best to provide their children with a secure, nurturing home? After all, addictions also arise in such families. The unseen factor here is the stress the parents themselves lived under, even if they did not recognize it. That stress could come from relationship problems or from outside circumstances such as economic pressure or political disruption.

The most frequent source of hidden stress is the parents' own childhood histories that saddle them with emotional baggage they are not conscious of. What we are not aware of in ourselves, we pass on to our children. Stressed, anxious, or depressed parents have

The Risk of Adult Substance Abuse Increases with More Adverse Childhood Experiences (ACEs)

Adverse childhood experiences (ACEs) are traumatic events such as neglect, physical or sexual abuse, and natural disasters, among others. As the number of ACEs someone has experienced increases, the prevalence of alcoholism or use of illicit drugs increases. The results regarding alcoholism were derived from researchers S.R. Dube et al. in a 2002 publication of *Addictive Behaviors*, and the illicit drugs results from S.R. Dube et al. in *Pediatrics* from 2003.

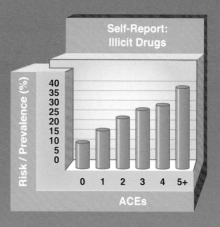

great difficulty initiating enough of those emotionally rewarding, endorphin-liberating interactions with their children. Later in life such children may experience a hit of heroin as the "warm, soft hug" my patient described: What they didn't get enough of before, they can now give themselves through a needle.

Unconditional Love and Acceptance

The U.S.-based Adverse Childhood Experiences studies have demonstrated beyond [a] doubt that childhood stresses, including factors such as abuse, addiction in the family, a rancorous divorce, and so on, provide the template for addictions later in life. It doesn't follow, of course, that all addicts were abused or that all abused children become addicts, but the correlations are inescapable.

If we look closely, we'll see that addictive patterns characterize the behaviors of many members of society, including high-functioning and respectable citizens. As a workaholic doctor, I've had my own non-substance addictions to feverish professional activity and also to shopping. In my case, I can trace that back to emotional losses I suffered as a Jewish infant in Nazi-occupied Hungary during the last years of World War II. My children, in turn, were subjected to the stresses of a family headed by a workaholic father who was physically present but emotionally absent.

Feeling alone, the sense that there has never been anyone with whom to share their deepest emotions, is universal among drug addicts. That is what Anna had lamented on her wall. No matter how much love a parent has, the child does not experience being wanted unless he or she is made absolutely safe to express exactly how unhappy, or angry, or hate-filled he or she may at times feel. The sense of unconditional love, of being fully accepted even when most ornery, is what no addict ever experienced in childhood—not because the parents did not have it to give, but simply because they were too stressed, or overworked, or beset by their own demons, or simply did not know how to transmit it to the child.

Addicts rarely make the connection between troubled childhood experiences and self-harming habits. They blame themselves—and that is the greatest wound of all, being cut off from their natural self-compassion. "I was hit a lot," 40-year-old Wayne told me, "but I asked for it. Then I made some stupid decisions." And would he hit a child, no matter how much that child "asked for it," or blame that child for "stupid decisions"? "I don't want to talk about that crap," said this tough man, who has worked on oil rigs and construction sites and served 15 years in jail for robbery. He looked away and wiped a tear from his eyes.

FIVE

Drug War Madness

Laura Carlsen

Laura Carlsen is a columnist for the think tank Foreign Policy in Focus and director of the Americas Program for the Center for International Policy in Mexico City. In the following viewpoint Carlsen argues that the war on drugs has failed and new strategies must be considered to address drug abuse. She says that attempting to control drug use with military tactics has resulted in negative consequences, such as a high imprisonment rate of US citizens. According to the author, the expansion of the drug war to other countries has had even more harmful effects, including an increase in drug-related violence. Carlsen notes that since the Merida Initiative—a joint US/Mexican program to counter drug trafficking through military means—began in 2007, nearly fifty thousand Mexicans have been killed in drug war violence, and hundreds of thousands more have been traumatized or forced to abandon their homes.

In 1936, a church group commissioned a film "to strike fear in the hearts of young people tempted to smoke marijuana." But it was not until the 1970s that *Reefer Madness*—billed as "the original classic that was not afraid to make up the truth" due to its grotesque portrayal of the supposed dangers of marijuana—obtained cult status.

After the scare tactics of the 1930s, U.S. marijuana policy varied depending on the political climate, even as scientific research consistently debunked extreme claims that the plant caused uncontrollable violent behavior, physical addiction, and insanity.

Then on June 17, 1971, President Richard Nixon launched his signature "war on drugs." The new crackdown on illegal drug use shifted the issue from a local health and public safety problem to a series of federal agencies under the direct control of the president. President Ronald Reagan later doubled down on the drug war, ushering in an age of mass incarceration.

Like the film before it, the drug war model not only criminalized but also demonized illegal drug dealing and use—and the individuals involved—in moralistic and military terms. In many states, selling marijuana carried longer sentences than murder. Although the abuse of legal drugs now kills more people than illegal drugs, the architects of the drug war continue to promote the view that it is some inherent evil of the substance, rather than the way individuals and groups use it, that determines whether a drug is a threat to society or an accepted social custom.

The Drug Policy Alliance has revealed that U.S. authorities arrest some 800,000 people a year for marijuana use. Two-thirds of those incarcerated in state prisons for drug offenses are black or Hispanic, even though consumption rates for whites are equal. Largely because of drug laws and draconian enforcement, the United States has become the world champion in imprisoning its own people, often destroying the hopes and futures of its youth. The United States spends more than $51 billion a year on the domestic war on drugs alone.

Exporting the War

The export version of the drug war has an even darker side. It makes the implicit racism of the domestic war overt. Foreign drug lords are stereotypically portrayed as the root of an evil enterprise that, in fact, takes place mostly in the United States, where street sales generate the multibillion-dollar profits of the business. Under the guise of the drug war, the U.S. government has sponsored military responses in other countries that the Constitution prohibits domestically—for good reasons.

Attention is diverted from the social roots of drug abuse and addiction at home to a foreign threat to the *American way of life*—a way of life that, regardless of one's moral beliefs, has always been characterized by the widespread use of mind-altering drugs. The false war model of good vs. evil, ally vs. enemy precludes many community-based solutions that have proven to be far more effective. U.S. taxpayers pay billions of dollars to fumigate foreign lands, pursue drug traffickers, and patrol borders as well as land and sea routes to intercept shipments.

None of this has worked. More than a decade and $8 billion into Plan Colombia, that Andean nation is the number-one cocaine producer in the world. Mexico has exploded into violence as the arrests and killings of cartel leaders spark turf battles that bathe whole regions in blood.

Last month, 52 people lost their lives in an attack on a casino in Monterrey, Mexico. The news shocked Mexico since it represents yet another escalation of violence, but it's become almost routine alongside daily drug-war deaths. For U.S. citizens, it was further proof that Mexico is under an assault by organized crime.

According to some Mexican researchers, the sudden rise in violence in Mexico correlates directly to when President Felipe Calderon launched his crackdown in the war on drugs by sending troops and federal police into the streets in 2006. Meanwhile, Mexican citizens have also taken to the streets to proclaim the war on drugs directly responsible for the growing bloodshed in their country and demand a change in strategy. Calderon has refused to consider alternative models.

Obama's Drug-War Failure

This year the Global Commission on Drug Policy released a report that concludes that "Political leaders and public figures should have the courage to articulate publicly what many of them acknowledge privately: that the evidence overwhelmingly demonstrates that repressive strategies will not solve the drug problem, and that the war on drugs has not, and cannot, be won."

A Majority of Americans Believe the Drug War Has Failed

In an online survey conducted by Angus Reid, a representative sample of Americans were asked, "From what you have seen, read, or heard, would you describe the 'war on drugs' as a success or a failure?"

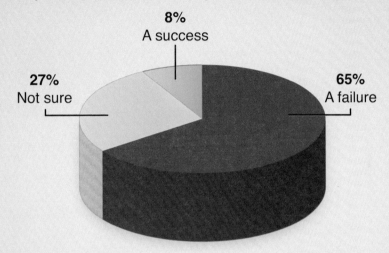

8%
A success

27%
Not sure

65%
A failure

Taken from: "Americans Decry War on Drugs, Blame Mexico for Allowing Cartels to Grow." Angus Reid Public Opinion, July 21, 2010. www.visioncritical.com/wp-content/uploads/2010/07/2010.21_Drugs_USA.pdf.

Instead, the Obama administration has added fist and firepower to the drug wars. Ignoring 40 years of policy failure, Obama has broken campaign promises to seek a more humane and effective drug policy. His administration has failed to support international harm reduction models, reversed a decision not to go after state medical marijuana regimes voted by popular referendums, reaffirmed marijuana's classification as a schedule 1 controlled substance with no medical value, and expanded drug wars in Mexico and Central America.

The government reprehensibly continues to expand the failed drug war in the face of the budget crisis and drastic cutbacks in schools, healthcare, and basic social programs. A good example is the multimillion-dollar boondoggle called the "Merida Initiative." Under this ill-conceived regional security cooperation measure,

The 1936 film Reefer Madness (advertised here) was an attempt "to strike fear in the hearts of young people tempted to smoke marijuana." An early propaganda piece, the film was a grotesque portrayal of the supposed dangers of marijuana that was full of inaccuracies and hyperbole.

the United States sends intelligence and defense equipment and provides military and police training for Mexico and, to a lesser degree, Central American countries. This drug-war strategy has increased violence in Mexico and led to a severe deterioration in public safety, rule of law, and human rights. The resources go to Mexican security forces notorious for corruption and even complicity with organized crime.

The results of the drug war in Mexico have been nothing short of catastrophic. Since it began, nearly 50,000 Mexicans have lost their lives in drug-war-related violence. Hundreds of thousands of people have been forced to leave their homes, children have been orphaned and traumatized, men, and thousands have been kidnapped and still missing.

The attacks on cartels—including the killing or capture of leaders—spark turf wars that rage throughout Mexico, with the worst concentrated along the northern border. In response, some cartels have reorganized, with splinter groups frequently employing far more violent tactics than their parent organizations. Military operations have pushed the violence around the country in what experts call a "whack-a-mole" strategy that shows no signs of letting up.

The invented threat of reefer madness has been replaced with the real disaster of *drug war madness*—government perseverance with lethal and ineffective policies. The drug war, with its exaggerated claims and mistaken focus on confronting drug trafficking with police and military force, has cost the United States and its targeted suppliers like Colombia and Mexico millions of dollars and thousands of lives.

In Mexico, a peace movement has arisen against the drug war. It has opened up dialogue with the government but been met with an absolute refusal to consider other options. In the United States, drug-policy reform turns up at the top of lists of issues for town-hall discussions, but politicians dismiss the issue because it's taboo or too risky for their political aspirations.

Policymakers must come to their senses regarding the madness of the drug-war strategy. If they don't voluntarily propose reforms, then citizens will have to force them to do so.

SIX

All Drugs Should Be Legalized

John Stossel

> John Stossel is a journalist, host of a weekly news show on Fox News, and former coanchor of the ABC TV documentary series *20/20*. In the following viewpoint Stossel argues that adults should have the right to decide what drugs they use and that therefore all drugs should be legal. According to the author, much of what is commonly believed about illegal drugs is exaggerated or untrue. For example, most people believe that everyone who uses drugs such as heroin and crack will become addicted, but Stossel cites statistics showing that most people who try crack do not continue to use it. Prohibition itself causes many of the harms associated with drugs, Stossel asserts; for example, making drugs so expensive that people must commit crimes to get the money to pay for them. He says prohibition does not work anyway, pointing out that drugs cannot even be kept out of prisons, let alone society at large.

The other day, reading the *New York Post*'s popular Page Six gossip page, I was surprised to find a picture of me, followed by the lines: "ABC's John Stossel wants the government to stop interfering with your right to get high. . . . The crowd went silent at his call to legalize hard drugs."

I had attended a Marijuana Policy Project event celebrating the New York State . . . Assembly's passage of a medical-marijuana bill. (The bill hasn't passed the Senate.) I told the audience I thought it pathetic that the mere half passage of a bill to allow sick people to try a possible remedy would merit such a celebration. *Of course* medical marijuana should be legal. For adults, *everything* should be legal. I'm amazed that the health police are so smug in their opposition.

After years of reporting on the drug war, I'm convinced that this "war" does more harm than any drug.

Those who advocate for the legalization of drugs say that the prohibition of drugs itself has caused many of the harms that have been associated with drug use.

Independent of that harm, adults ought to own our own bodies, so it's not intellectually honest to argue that "only marijuana" should be legal—and only for certain sick people approved by the state. Every drug should be legal.

"How could you say such a ridiculous thing?" asked my assistant. "Heroin and cocaine have a permanent effect. If you do crack just once, you are automatically hooked. Legal hard drugs would create many more addicts. And that leads to more violence, homelessness, out-of-wedlock births, etc!"

Her diatribe is a good summary of the drug warriors' arguments. Most Americans probably agree with what she said.

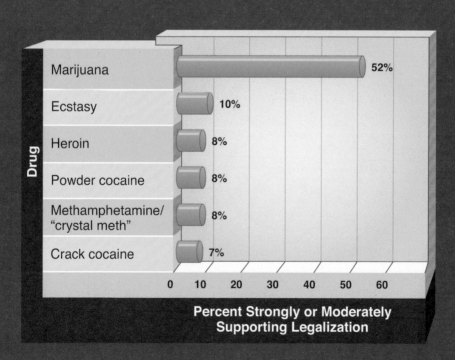

Percent of Americans Favoring Legalization of Various Drugs

Marijuana — 52%
Ecstasy — 10%
Heroin — 8%
Powder cocaine — 8%
Methamphetamine/ "crystal meth" — 8%
Crack cocaine — 7%

Drug

0 10 20 30 40 50 60

Percent Strongly or Moderately Supporting Legalization

Taken from: "Americans Decry War on Drugs, Blame Mexico for Allowing Cartels to Grow." Angus Reid Public Opinion, July 21, 2010. www.visioncritical.com/wp-content/uploads/2010/07/2010.07.21_Drugs_USA.pdf.

The Dangers of Drugs Are Exaggerated

But what most Americans believe is wrong.

Myth No. 1: Heroin and cocaine have a permanent effect.

Truth: There is no evidence of that.

In the 1980s, the press reported that "crack babies" were "permanently damaged." *Rolling Stone*, citing one study of just 23 babies, claimed that crack babies "were oblivious to affection, automatons."

It simply wasn't true. There is no proof that crack babies do worse than anyone else in later life.

Myth No. 2: If you do crack once, you are hooked.

Truth: Look at the numbers—15 percent of young adults have tried crack, but only 2 percent used it in the last month. If crack is so addictive, why do most people who've tried it no longer use it?

People once said heroin was nearly impossible to quit, but during the Vietnam War, thousands of soldiers became addicted, and when they returned home, 85 percent quit within one year.

People have free will. Most who use drugs eventually wise up and stop.

And most people who use drugs habitually live perfectly responsible lives, as Jacob Sullum pointed out in "Saying Yes."

Myth No. 3: Drugs cause crime.

Truth: The drug *war* causes the crime.

Few drug users hurt or rob people because they are high. Most of the crime occurs *because* the drugs are illegal and available only through a black market. Drug sellers arm themselves and form gangs because they cannot ask the police to protect their persons and property.

In turn, some buyers steal to pay the high black-market prices. The government says heroin, cocaine and nicotine are similarly addictive, and about half the people who both smoke cigarettes and use cocaine say smoking is at least as strong an urge. But no one robs convenience stores for Marlboros.

The Harm Caused by Prohibition

Alcohol prohibition created [gangster] Al Capone and the Mafia. Drug prohibition is worse. It's corrupting whole countries and financing terrorism.

The *Post* wrote, "Stossel admitted his own 22-year-old daughter doesn't think [legalization] is a good idea."

But that's not what she said. My daughter argued that legal cocaine would probably lead to more cocaine use. And therefore probably abuse.

I'm not so sure.

Banning drugs certainly hasn't kept young people from getting them. We can't even keep these drugs out of prisons. How do we expect to keep them out of America?

But let's assume my daughter is right, that legalization would lead to more experimentation and more addiction. I still say: Legal is better.

While drugs harm many, the drug war's black market harms more.

And most importantly, in a free country, adults should have the right to harm themselves.

SEVEN

Effective Education Programs Are Successful in Preventing Drug Abuse

The Economist

The *Economist* is a weekly international news and business publication founded in London, England, in 1843. Its editorial policy eschews the use of bylines for its writers. In the following viewpoint the *Economist* argues that the key to reducing the harms associated with drug abuse is to persuade people not to use them in the first place. It notes a strong correlation between how harmful a drug is perceived to be by young people and how likely they are to use it; for example, in the 1980s there was a significant reduction in cocaine use among twelfth-grade students—even though the drug was easier to get—because of increased student perception of its harmfulness. According to the authors, drug education approaches that inform students of long-term effects of drug abuse tend to have little impact. Instead, it has been found that giving accurate information about short-term adverse consequences—for example, that users of methamphetamine tend to have rotten teeth, or that tobacco smokers are less popular—is much more effective.

His memories are addled, but the young member of Cocaine Anonymous can just about recall his formal drug education. When he was about 11, he says, a police officer made several visits to his school to give warning of the dangers posed by illicit substances. Although he remembers thinking the cop was "something of a Dudley-Do-Right" he agreed with him that drugs were best avoided. He recalls no further lessons. By his late teens he was addicted to crack cocaine and methamphetamine.

By far the best way of reducing the harm that drugs can do is to convince people not to take them. Spraying crops, seizing shipments and arresting dealers can drive up prices and create temporary shortages. But it does not stop drug use. Addicts simply pay more for crummier product or switch to other, often more harmful, substances. Cocaine-takers may move to powder amphetamine or crystal meth; heroin addicts experiment with oxycodone. "It's like a water-bed. Push down in one place and another drug pops up," says Rod Skager, who surveys teenagers' drug-taking for the California state government.

Perceptions of Harm

In the late 1980s cocaine-taking fell steeply among 12th-grade pupils—that is, 17- and 18-year-olds—according to the University of Michigan's long-running Monitoring the Future survey. Those teenagers reported that the drug was more available than ever. They had simply decided not to take it on the grounds that it was harmful. The same thing happened with ecstasy earlier in this decade. Given the strong link between perceptions of harm and use, it is a bad sign that attitudes to cocaine are again becoming rather relaxed.

Most attempts to reduce drug demand in America are aimed at 11- to 14-year-olds. The principle is that children should be reached while they are still fairly pliable and before they begin to take drugs—not just the hard stuff but alcohol, marijuana and tobacco. The hope is that they will develop a broad aversion to harmful substances that will stay with them through their late teens and early 20s, when drug use peaks. Only when an

The approach to preventing drug abuse that the Drug Abuse Resistance Education (DARE) program uses has been a favorite of parents because they think their children will listen to and be influenced by the testimonies of police officers and celebrities.

immensely damaging drug emerges suddenly, as crystal meth did in some western states a few years ago, are concerted efforts made to communicate with older teenagers.

Until recently the dominant approach was Drug Abuse Resistance Education (DARE), a programme developed in Los Angeles in 1983 and quickly exported to the rest of America. Cops would arrive in schools, sometimes driving cars confiscated from drug-dealers, and tell 11- and 12-year-olds about the dangers of illicit substances. They drew little or no distinction between marijuana and methamphetamine. Teachers liked DARE because they felt uncomfortable tackling the topic themselves, and because they got a break. Parents liked it because they felt their children would listen to police officers.

Changing Approaches to Drug Education

Unfortunately, they did not. A string of academic studies labelled DARE pointless at best. Some academics and former drug-takers—argue that efforts to scare young children about drugs that they may not have heard of are actually counter-

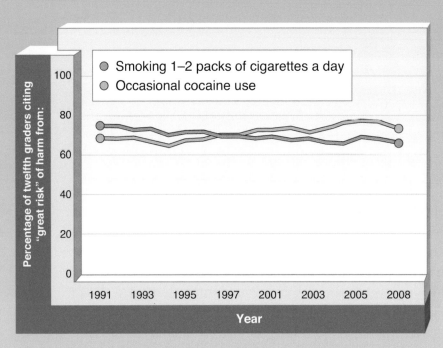

A Shift in Teenagers' Perceptions of Drug Use

- Smoking 1–2 packs of cigarettes a day
- Occasional cocaine use

Percentage of twelfth graders citing "great risk" of harm from:

y-axis: 0, 20, 40, 60, 80, 100

x-axis (Year): 1991 1993 1995 1997 2001 2003 2005 2008

These results were collected by Monitoring the Future.

Taken from: "In America, Lessons Learned." *The Economist*, March 5, 2009. www.economist.com/node/13234144/.

productive. "They're a challenge," says Taylor, a Los Angeles native who is recovering from an addiction to crack cocaine and heroin. The federal government opted not to pay for the programme. It survives (DARE claims it is still used in 72% of America's school districts), but in an altered form. It has even been dropped by the Los Angeles school district, where it began.

The new approach to drug education, reflected in the remodelled DARE, is more oblique. By means of role-playing, cops and teachers try to provide children with the confidence to resist pressures of all kinds, from drugs to internet bullying. Rather than telling children that drugs are dangerous, teachers assure them that they are rare. Drugs are no longer treated as a unique, self-contained threat—which indeed they are often not. "Kids do not normally walk in with a drug problem who do not have other problems," says Lori Vollandt, who co-ordinates health programmes in Los Angeles' schools.

The new programmes are mostly intended to reduce alcohol, marijuana and tobacco use, and are evaluated in those terms. There is a good reason for that. Because they are so widespread, the total harm caused to teenagers by alcohol and tobacco is much greater than the total harm caused by harder drugs. There is also a less good reason. Educators worry about the "boomerang effect", in which talk about drugs feeds curiosity about them.

Improving the Message

The success of the campaign against methamphetamine suggests the boomerang effect is overdone, at least for older teenagers. Meth is an old drug that suddenly became popular again in the late 1990s. It is generally made by cooking ammonia, lithium and pseudoephedrine, a decongestant. The manufacturing process is extremely dangerous and the finished product hardly safer. Faced with an epidemic, Montana and other western states rolled out advertising campaigns. But rather than emphasise the drug's addictiveness and long-term effects on the brain, as earlier anti-drug campaigns had done, these pointed out that meth users often had rotten teeth. It worked: in the past five years attitudes to the drug have hardened and use has dropped steeply.

Even greater success has been achieved against tobacco. Since the mid-1990s, the proportion of 12th-grade pupils who believe smoking a packet or two of cigarettes a day carries a great risk has risen by about ten percentage points. Regular puffing on cigarettes is now thought much more dangerous than occasionally smoking crack.

There are several reasons for this. Hollywood has virtually stopped glamorizing cigarettes. Executives have been shamed and smokers ostracised. But a big reason is that the people who create anti-tobacco ads have refined their messages. They now know, for example, that warnings about long-term health effects do not scare teenagers. The long-term is too far off. Pointing out that second-hand smoke can harm babies turns out to work. So do ads suggesting that non-smokers are more popular.

It may seem odd that the campaign against tobacco, a legal drug, has displayed so much more élan than the war on illegal drugs. Yet this is natural. Making a drug illegal may discourage some people from taking it, but it also discourages frank conversation and clear thinking. It is much easier to attack something if it is brought into the light.

EIGHT

Spiritual Meaning Is Needed to Combat Drug Abuse

Jeremy Egerer

Jeremy Egerer is a recent convert to Christian conservatism from radical liberalism and is the editor of the Seattle website American Clarity. In the following viewpoint Egerer argues that people turn to drug abuse because modern society teaches children that life is meaningless. He shares his own experiences of drug use, explaining that he felt unlovable and lost his faith in God, then turned to drugs like LSD and cocaine in an attempt to find companionship and acceptance. According to Egerer, the message that young people get from modern society is that there is no purpose, that there is nothing to truly believe in, and that they are fundamentally alone. Such pervasive messages of despair lead some young people to seek comfort in the false promises of drugs, in his view. What is needed to stop people from succumbing to drug abuse, he claims, is a sense of higher purpose and meaning that gives people something to live for.

I can still vividly remember walking through run-down Neapolitan [in Naples, Italy,] suburbs as a seventeen-year old, firmly within the grasp of an LSD trip. As I walked through the tall, unkempt grass and weeds, they brushed against my knees as though greeting me with a handshake. The summer sun was looking down upon me, and the rays felt as though they were shining into my body, as though I was illuminated and radiating life back into the universe. Though I usually noticed the garbage on the messy Italian streets, that day it seemed less prominent, if not unnoticeable, and nature's Technicolor vibrancy jumped from objects which would have been previously considered not only ordinary, but also drab. I was—at least I felt as though I were—totally connected with reality, as though something that I had lost along the way had suddenly been found, and I was home.

Explaining an LSD trip to someone who hasn't experienced one usually invokes wonder or disgust, but it's what really happens, at least in the psychedelic adventurer's head. To make things more exciting for me as a young man, this transfer of consciousness into transcendental bliss had come after a hard year of disillusionment. A home-schooler raised by devout Christian parents (whom I never deserved) and having experienced Christ, I had decided, though never quite entirely, that God didn't exist. To make things worse, aside from losing a caring Creator, I had always felt as though I would never be loved by anyone outside my family. I'd spent much time fantasizing about meeting the woman of my dreams, but my excessive weight problem, certain personal abnormalities, and problems with anxiety made me feel as though I would die a lonely man. And this crushed my spirit.

False Promises

When I sought drugs, I did so primarily to fit in with the cool kids so I could boost my status and find a mate. Sometimes, I felt as though I was on the verge of success. Late nights on ecstasy, [my] bonding with "friends" and women who would disappear when the high wore off, oftentimes gave the momentary impression that I wasn't alone, that I was accepted. It was as though I could talk, and others would listen. I could hug, and profess love, and not be turned away. I could meet new people, and they would instantly appreciate me.

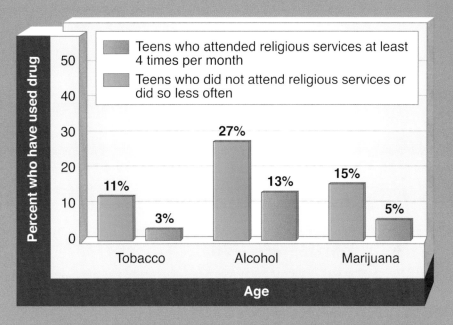

Attending Religious Services and Teen Drug Abuse

Percent who have used drug

- Teens who attended religious services at least 4 times per month
- Teens who did not attend religious services or did so less often

Tobacco: 11%, 3%
Alcohol: 27%, 13%
Marijuana: 15%, 5%

Age

Taken from: "Teen Risk of Substance Abuse and Attending Religious Services." National Survey of American Attitudes on Substance Abuse XVI: Teens and Parents. The National Center on Addiction and Substance Abuse at Columbia University (CASA), August 2011, p. 4. www.casacolumbia.org/upload/2011/20110824teensurveyreport.pdf.

But my eventual addiction to cocaine, Klonopins [clonazepam, used to treat seizures], and tequila, in combination with an emasculating yet trendy college liberalism, ironically made me unappealing to any women who would have been good partners. By the end of my drug habit, I was alone more than ever. I felt useless, unattractive, sleazy, and many times, I would have preferred to be dead. And although the lie of drugs should have become more clear to me—that the promises it made, that I would be cool, that women would love me, that I would find peace through intoxication, had dissipated further into the air with every puff from a bong—I clung harder to drugs out of desperation. I would wake up some mornings plastered to my pillow with my own blood, the product of ruptured nasal passages [from snorting cocaine].

Sometimes, I would swallow dangerous amounts of medications, just to see how high I could get without dying. Although I was walking, breathing, and capable of looking you right in the eyes and saying that things were fine—and maybe you might believe that I was doing well—behind my smiling face was a hollow shell, completely devoid of life and joy.

I don't believe I was ever alone in this desperation. In all the years I spent as a drug addict, I'm surprised to have never discovered this. I guess the fact that I was on drugs is a valid excuse. But I now know there were many others around me who were in the same position as I was, crying for help but unable to say so without looking too vulnerable. We were trying to be cool, after all. And coolness was killing us.

The Meaningless Void

But what my experience with drug addiction taught me, first and foremost, is that drug-smuggling Mexicans aren't the drug problem, and they aren't causing the drug problem. Please don't misunderstand my point: they're a menace to our society, and they must be combated with utmost seriousness (I personally advocate properly sealing the border and the death penalty for anyone who deals methamphetamine or heroin or is caught laundering serious drug money). But if we are to be at all serious about saving people from the horrors of human abasement, those very people must have something to live for greater than momentary pleasure. They must have hope. But hope in what?

Liberals are wrong when they say that giving a kid a chance at an education will accomplish this task. You give an empty, lonely, directionless, hurting person—a potential drug addict—an education, and all you've got is an educated drug addict. We can't combat drug abuse with feel-good rhetoric and can-do attitude, because hope in careers can take you only so far, and the warmth of philanthropy fades. Many of us know, despite what some may say, that placing our meaning entirely in the United States of America will end in anger and frustration. And we definitely know, after forty years, a trillion dollars, and numerous lives spent on the War against Drugs, that we can't win the war with the sword.

Now consider what we tell our children, as public policy. We tell them that they are alone in the universe, that their lives have absolutely no impact upon the great void. We tell them that everything they fight for, everything they believe in, is a postmodern matter of opinion. We tell them that pleasure is their right, and yet that as they age, they will receive less pleasure, and more pain, and that they cannot reverse this process. We tell them that marriage doesn't work anymore, that true love, true commitment doesn't exist, and that they can't trust the people whom they should trust the most. And finally, we fill the void with tons of useless products and entertainment and psychologically-manipulative advertising campaigns about what happiness should be and where we can get it with our paychecks, all illusory things which most—if not all—will never achieve.

Now allow me to ask you: is this what you tell someone whose self-destructive habit you want to reverse? Or is this what you say when you want them to hit the gas pedal? I know—placing ourselves in these terms isn't an uplifting message. But this is who we are, and this is what we tell our children. We are a consumptive, meaningless people without a Creator, without a purpose other than ourselves, and heading toward an eventually painful decay and death.

A Sense of Purpose

You should probably know that I have been clean and sober for quite some time now, that I've found and committed myself to the woman of my dreams, and above all else, that I've placed my life in the hands of my Creator. These days, although at times I remember the acid trip fondly, although I occasionally wonder how easy writing would be if I just had a line of coke, I have found joy and hope, so these thoughts fade into nothing. I know where I am going when I die, I know whom I serve, and I know what love is. My life has meaning, which is far more than I know most people—especially drug addicts—have. And this joy has completely replaced my need for escape, my desire for intoxication. These days, thankfully, I can enjoy a beer and know I won't spiral into an inebriated hell-ride.

A man at a drug rehabilitation program that uses a faith-based approach studies his Bible. Some people attribute widespread drug abuse to a lack of spirituality in American society.

Please don't misunderstand me. Drug addicts are not victims—they are responsible for their behavior. Without understanding this principle of personal responsibility, that who you are and your temporary chemical makeup do not determine your status under the law, we wouldn't have a real system of justice. But behind the responsibility must lie a *reason* to want something other than pleasure, something other than an escape. And if we citizens of the United States of America—one of the most drug-hungry populations—expect that the people who represent our values in office are going to somehow deliver us from a terrible soul-cancer, we are wrong. We have to start with giving the individual soul hope.

I have an answer to the void: it is purpose. My question to you is, what do you have to offer your children so they can live for something better than an easily accessible, temporary escape from nihilism? If we haven't got an answer, then I would say the war on drugs has already been lost.

NINE

Straightening the Irish Out About Addiction

Stanton Peele

> Stanton Peele is an expert on addiction who has received a Lifetime Achievement Award from the Drug Policy Alliance. He is the author of *7 Tools to Beat Addiction* and *The Truth About Addiction and Recovery* and posts frequently on his website, http://peele.net/. In the following viewpoint Peele argues that encouraging young people to abstain totally from using alcohol or other drugs increases problematic patterns of abuse and addiction. A better approach, he says, is to encourage responsible patterns of use. Focusing on alcohol as an example, Peele says that people in Ireland are very unlikely to drink alcohol on a daily basis, but have a very high rate of binge drinking (consuming large amounts of alcohol on one occasion)— whereas in Italy, where people often drink on a daily basis, binge drinking is rare. According to Peele, it is more effective to teach people to avoid harmful patterns of drug use, rather than seeking to eliminate use altogether.

I write from Killarney, where yesterday I delivered the keynote address at a conference on "Addiction-Proofing Our Communities." The conference opened with a speech by Ireland's drug czar, Desmond Corrigan, an academic pharmacologist who, unlike his American counterpart, provided hard data and humility. Nonetheless, he still communicated an unbalanced and inaccurate image of drugs, one destined to exacerbate the problem. (Oddly, the czar indicated this was true in the past, when he had predicted drops in drug use, following which drug use in fact increased. As a result, he said, "I no longer make predictions.")

That night, I asked Dr. Corrigan to examine his own data showing that, of all those in Ireland who had ever tried illicit drugs (cocaine, heroin, marijuana, mushrooms, meth), ten percent or fewer currently used them (the data are similar here). Of course, this image is totally at odds with what the czar was trying to communicate: that drugs are an irresistible scourge that human beings cannot control and must avoid at all costs. When I asked him to explain the results, he said, "people quit when they get jobs, have families, and mature. Actually, they tell us 'I simply didn't wish to continue using'."

I then directed his attention to the remarkably skewed usage patterns his data showed. While illicit drug use was largely self-limiting, pharmaceutical drug use, drinking, and smoking were not. (Although the Irish use fewer illicit drugs than us [Americans]—about a quarter have used one in their lives, compared with half of Americans—a higher percentage currently drink—about three quarters, compared with half of Americans.) The czar answered by indicating that, although his province was only drugs, they intended to become as heavy-handed with alcohol as they already are with drugs. "Based on the work of Robin Room, we are arguing to raise the drinking age from 18 to 21, and to tax alcohol heavily."

By the time my speech rolled around the next day, of course, the czar was long gone. I noted that it would have been stressful for him to listen to my talk, and I appointed one of the conference organizers to stand in his stead. In my own imitable style, interacting with the czar stand-in, I then made the following points:

Given that his mission was to reduce drug use, it was remarkable that he did not note that the vast majority of people do so on their own, and (until I asked him) why and how they did so.

In Ireland a survey of teenagers aged fifteen to nineteen found that more than 50 percent frequently drank heavily and that a similar number had tried illegal drugs. The author claims it is more responsible to drink moderate amounts daily than to binge weekly.

I told the "czar" that he was disingenuous when he said he no longer made predictions—"You are here predicting the steps you are taking will improve the situation."

I then turned to the audience (by now on the edge of their seats) to ask what it meant that the czar's predictions were previously disproved, and they correctly shouted out—"He has failed." And so, I pointed out, "he is now proposing more of the same." (Of course, the Irish drug czar is worlds apart from his American counterpart, for example in endorsing methadone, needle exchange, and other harm reduction techniques that can only be employed sub rosa in the U.S.)

I then pointed out that the Irish—like Americans—were tremendously culturally ambivalent about alcohol. I cited data showing that Irish men are the least likely to drink daily (2%) and most likely to binge once weekly (roughly half) in Europe.

These data are almost exactly reversed for Italian men, who have high daily drinking rates, but rarely binge. I then reviewed data showing that three percent of Italian youth binge drink three or more times a month, compared with a quarter of Irish youth—the highest figure in Europe.

To his stand-in, I then said, "So what do you think you will accomplish by imposing more restrictive alcohol regulations? By the way, do you drink? And how did you introduce your children to alcohol?" His stand-in admitted that both he and the czar drank wine with meals, and had taught this custom to their children. Of course, this is the approach Italians take (the drinking age in Italy is 16, and parents can give children of any age alcohol at a restaurant).

"So, I said, you feel the best approach for you and those you love is mild social drinking, and teaching this to youngsters, but for the Irish at large, you intend to raise the drinking age and make it harder for them to afford alcohol; in other words, they can't be expected to learn the healthy patterns you yourself practice."

I continued, "And by how much do you realistically expect to lower the prevalence of Irish drinkers (90% of whom have imbibed)? Of course, what you will really accomplish is to exacerbate the ambivalence and uncertainty with which the Irish already drink, so that you can come back in future years to admit how you failed in this area also."

At this point, I stepped back and said to the "czar," "I understand—as the Chairperson of the National Advisory Committee on Drugs—you are primarily concerned with drugs. Really, what this means (as it does for the director of the American National Institute on Drug Abuse—with whom I would never be permitted to share a venue) is that you must constantly terrorize people about illicit drug use. On the other hand, examining your data—showing fewer than five percent of the Irish use marijuana, .5% use cocaine, and '0.0%' (actual figure) use heroin, while much higher percentages use a pharmaceutical

(10% use sedatives and a similar number anti-depressants) while three-quarters drink, the Irish people are not getting good value from paying your salary. (Recently, in the U.S., the head of the NIDA—Nora Volkow—following as she always does my insights but years later—has labeled pharmaceutical abuse as the number one drug problem in America.)

"I, on the other hand, am the sole member of the Intergalactic Commission on Addiction. I am only interested in harmful substance use, not with banning or discouraging use of disapproved

Spectrum of Psychoactive Substance Use

This diagram was adapted from BC Ministry of Health Services, "Every Door Is the Right Door: A British Columbia Planning Framework to Address Problematic Substance Use and Addiction," 2004.

Casual/Non-Problematic Use
* Recreational or other use that has negligible health or social impact.

Chronic Dependence
* Use that has become habitual and compulsive despite negative health and social impacts.

Beneficial Use
* Use that has positive health or social impact.
* e.g., medical psyshopharmaceuticals; coffee to increase alertness; moderate consumption of red wine; sacramental use of ayahuasca or peyote (derived from psychoactive plants).

Problematic Use
* Use that begins to have negative consequences for individual, friends/family, or society.
* e.g., impaired driving; binge consumption; harmful routes of administration.

substances. So let us speak here today about how we can best aid our children in avoiding harmful substance use, and addictions of all kind (the audience immediately agreed that addiction was not limited to drugs and alcohol)."

Of course, everywhere—even the countries like Ireland and the UK, closest to the U.S. in their screwy attitudes toward alcohol and drugs—there is greater diversity of opinion permitted on the subject of drugs. I was invited by a group in Kerry County who teach "Life Education" in the schools (none of whom would at all agree with my remarks to the czar!)—their mission is "to help children make healthy choices." You can see already why they would have me, creator of the Life Process Program, come to speak. We both agree that the key to avoiding unhealthy substance use, along with all addiction, is to encourage positive life attitudes and to arm young people with the knowledge and skill to live such a life.

In the U.S., where education programs are called "Drug Prevention," meaning their mission is to say the scariest things possible at all times about both drugs and alcohol, there is no room for my voice at all. Thus I will be speaking in London and Paris shortly—in France addressing the national association of substance abuse counsellors. But you will never hear my voice in Washington, D.C.

TEN

Prescription Drug Abuse Is a Growing Problem

Jeneba Ghatt

Jeneba Ghatt is a journalist, speaker, attorney, and founding member and policy chair for the National Association of Multicultural Digital Entrepreneurs. In the following viewpoint Ghatt argues that prescription drug abuse is a large and growing problem, particularly among young people and women. She says that one in five people in the United States have used prescription medication for non-medical purposes, including about 6 million people aged twelve or older in 2004. According to the author, women are especially vulnerable to prescription drug abuse, due to various factors, including a greater likelihood of suffering trauma and depression, which are associated with drug abuse, as well as being much more often prescribed drugs that are frequently abused (e.g., antianxiety medication and narcotic drugs). She asserts that other factors are exacerbating the problem, such as strong marketing efforts by the pharmaceutical industry and an increase in Internet pharmacies providing abusable medical drugs without proper safeguards.

The curious circumstances of [pop singer] Whitney Houston's death [on February 11, 2012,] are causing those fighting against drugs to revisit prescription drug abuse among women and, in particular, mothers.

Although the Los Angeles County Coroner's office is yet to release final toxicology and autopsy results to confirm whether prescription drugs were in Houston's body at the time of death, several reports indicate that there were bottles of Xanax [an anti-anxiety medicine] and other prescription pain relievers in her hotel room on the day she died.

The National Survey on Drug Use and Health found that nearly 6 million persons twelve years and older used psychotherapeutic and/or painkilling drugs for recreational purposes in 2004, representing 2.5 percent of the US population.

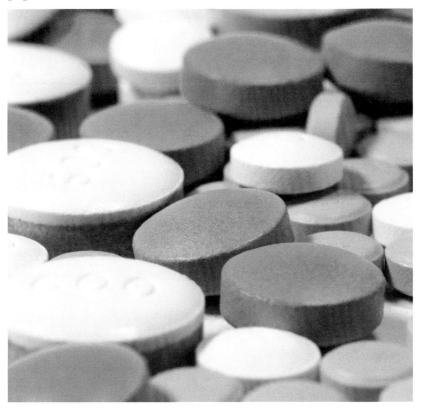

When people think of drugs, they traditionally think of street drugs like marijuana, cocaine, heroin, methamphetamines, and even alcohol, usually overlooking prescription drugs, such as the opiates, benzodiazepines, tranquilizers and others.

This drug class includes narcotic painkillers like OxyContin or Vicodin, sedatives and tranquilizers like Xanax or Valium at one spectrum end, and stimulants like Dexedrine, Adderall or Ritalin at the other.

All are physically and mentally addictive. All can have devestating results, including death, when the drugs are mixed, and/or drugs are taken with alcohol.

A first introduction to these addictive drugs often follows an injury or surgery; their purpose is to help the patient, under doctor's supervision, cope with pain.

Commonly Abused Painkillers and Sedatives

Narcotics Anonymous reports that people can build a tolerance to the effect of opiates fairly quickly.

Attesting to their mis-use, prescription drugs are the second most commonly abused category of drugs, behind marijuana and ahead of cocaine, heroin, methamphetamine and other drugs. The National Institutes of Health [NIH] estimates that nearly 20 percent of people in the United States have used prescription drugs for non-medical reasons.

A National Survey on Drug Use and Health revealed that approximately 6 million persons 12 and older used psychotherapeutic drugs for non-medical purposes in 2004, which represents 2.5 percent of the U.S. population.

In 2000, about 43 percent of hospital emergency admissions for drug overdoses (nearly 500,000 people) happened because of misused prescription drugs. The problem is prevalent among teens as well.

The number of teens and young adults (ages 12 to 25) who were new abusers of prescription painkillers grew from 400,000 in the mid-'80s to 2 million in 2000, according to a study by the Substance Abuse and Mental Health Services Administration.

Even before children enter their teens, the modern world insistence on medicating children for attention deficit disorder and other psychological disorders has led to children's developing a dependency on sedative type drugs. Among 12th graders, in 2005, 9.5% reported past-year non-medical use of Vicodin, and 5.5% reported past-year non-medical use of OxyContin, according to the NIH Substance Abuse Study.

Especially Problematic for Women

Sadly, women in particular are vulnerable.

The then director of the National Institute on Drug Abuse at NIH, Nora D. Volkow, M.D., testified in 2006 before The Subcommittee on Criminal Justice, Drug Policy, and Human Resources Committee on Government Reform in the U.S. House of Representatives.

"Prescription drug abuse must also be carefully tracked among women because of their combined vulnerabilities," she said. "First, women are more likely than men to suffer from depression, anxiety, trauma, and victimization, all of which frequently appear with substance abuse in the form of co-morbidities [other illnesses suffered along with the primary one]."

Volkow added that "girls and women report using drugs to cope with stressful situations in their lives" and that "studies suggest that women are significantly more likely than men to be prescribed an abusable drug, particularly in the form of narcotics and anti-anxiety medications."

It is an issue even among pregnant women. A study published in the *American Journal of Obstetrics & Gynecology* [reported that] around half of all moms-to-be now take at least one medication.

Often times, society paints drug abuse as a problem of the poor, but in fact, affluent and middle-income women and college students are among the most prevalent abusers of prescription drugs.

A 2009 news report expressed surprise that well-to-do housewives and college students were the leading abusers of prescription

While overdose deaths from heroin remained fairly constant between 1999 and 2009, overdose deaths caused by opioid-based prescription drugs increased dramatically. Some overdose deaths may have been counted twice if both opioid-based prescription drugs and heroin were involved. These figures were derived from the Centers for Disease Control and Prevention.

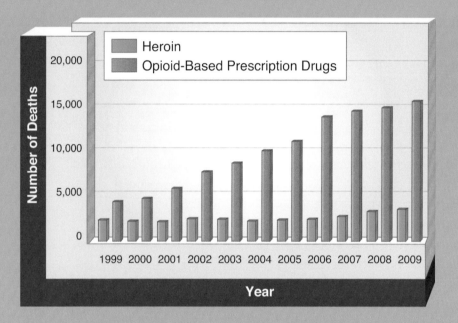

Taken from: Lam Thuy Vo/NPR. www.npr.org/blogs/money/2012/07/26/155424108/meet-the-drug-dealer-who-helps -addicts-quit.

drugs. It quoted Fresno County [California] Coroner Dr. David Hadden who noted that "the 'it' pills are hydrocodone, which include vicodin and norco, morphine, and now the most popular pain pill of choice, OxyContin" and pointed out that many of the 81 people who died that year "had a cocktail of drugs in their system when they died, like mixing painkillers, with cocaine and methamphetamine, or sedatives and alcohol."

A Growing Problem

Because of the demand, prescription drugs on the black market are expensive. On the street, one pill can cost as high as $40 to $50.

The issue is certainly not new, A 1973 study in the *Journal of Drug Education* spoke about how middle-class housewives were physician shopping to get one that would prescribe drugs.

Today, the NIH notes that access is even easier, pointing out, among other factors, that "aggressive marketing by the pharmaceutical industry, the proliferation of illegal Internet pharmacies that dispense these medications without proper prescriptions and surveillance and a greater social acceptability for medicating a growing number of conditions."

Some states, like New Jersey, are cracking down by launching investigations and surveillance efforts to root out how prescription pills enter the black market trade in the first place, whether by indiscriminate prescribing, unlawful distribution and/or theft of prescription blanks. The federal government continues to conduct research studies into how to prevent and treat abuse, but meanwhile the problem seems to be worsening.

It all leaves one to wonder whether enough is being done, however. After [actor] Heath Ledger, [celebrity] Ana Nicole Smith and now, possibly, Whitney Houston, may have met their deaths due to the misuse of prescription medication, one would think such high-profile deaths would be sufficient for government initiatives to combat the problem.

Hopefully, Houston's death may lead to more outcry and inquiry into the problem. We cannot afford to lose many more teens, or mothers to prescription drug abuse.

ELEVEN

Attempts to Prevent People from Abusing Prescription Drugs Are Harming Legitimate Users

Jacob Sullum

Jacob Sullum is a senior editor at *Reason* magazine, a nationally syndicated columnist, and the author of *Saying Yes: In Defense of Drug Use* and *For Your Own Good: The Anti-Smoking Crusade and the Tyranny of Public Health*. In the following viewpoint Sullum argues that attempts to reduce nonmedical abuse of prescription painkillers are harming legitimate medical users of such drugs. According to Sullum, most nonmedical users get their drugs from relatives or friends who have prescriptions, so any successful reduction in the supply of such drugs would inevitably involve legitimate users' being deprived of their medicine. The author claims that attempts to require doctors to get special training to discriminate between legitimate and illegitimate use would make them more suspicious of *all* patients (including legitimate users) and would also reduce the number of doctors who were authorized to prescribe narcotic medication. People who need painkillers should not be deprived of them because others use them inappropriately, he concludes.

Last week [in April 2011], unveiling a plan to curtail "diversion" of opioid painkillers, [Barack] Obama administration officials said they aim to "strike a balance between our desire to minimize abuse of prescription drugs and the need to ensure access for their legitimate use." This balance will never be achieved because the two goals are fundamentally irreconcilable.

Since pain cannot be verified objectively, there is only so much a conscientious doctor can do to make sure a patient is not a malingerer, an addict, or a drug dealer. At a certain point, he has to choose between trusting his patients and helping the

A California doctor uses a computer database to check a patient's history before prescribing a painkiller. The Barack Obama administration wants every state to establish such monitoring programs and to share the information collected to help avoid prescription-drug abuse.

government enforce its arbitrary dictates regarding psychoactive chemicals. If he sides with his patients, he risks his license, his livelihood, and his liberty. If he sides with the government, it is inevitable that some patients will suffer needlessly.

Discouraging Legitimate Use

Doctors are less inclined to prescribe opioids, even to legitimate patients in horrible pain, when they worry that regulators, police, and federal drug agents are looking over their shoulders, ready to second-guess every decision and transform honest mistakes or medical disagreements into felonies. Every additional layer of scrutiny only compounds the drug war's chilling effect on pain treatment.

That is one of the problems with the computerized prescription drug monitoring programs (PDMPs) that the Obama administration wants every state to establish. The benefits of such programs, which 35 states have implemented so far, are questionable. A recent study by researchers at the U.S. Centers for Disease Control and Prevention found that "PDMP states did not do any better than non-PDMP states in controlling the rise in drug overdose mortality from 1999 to 2005."

To the extent that PDMPs do succeed in changing doctors' prescribing practices, the impact won't be limited to nonmedical users. Data from the National Survey on Drug Use and Health indicate that 70 percent of nonmedical users get painkillers from friends or relatives with prescriptions. Cutting off these sources through aggressive monitoring is bound to hurt many legitimate patients.

The same thing is true of the Obama administration's proposed requirement that doctors be barred from prescribing narcotic painkillers until they receive "training on the importance of appropriate prescribing and dispensing of opioids to prevent adverse effects, diversion, and addiction." First, the training mandate (which would require new legislation) would reduce legitimate patients' access to painkillers by reducing the number of physicians authorized to prescribe them. Second, the focus of

Many Americans suffer from conditions that produce chronic pain. In 2011, 47 percent of Americans surveyed said they will suffer from at least one of the three pain conditions depicted in this visual; 7 percent suffer from all three. Measures that strictly control access to pain control medication may mean reduced access for those who need it for legitimate reasons.

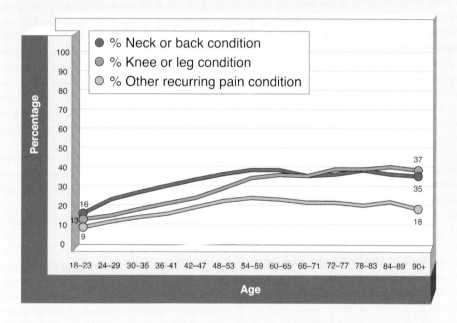

Taken from: Gallup-Healthways Well-Being Index, 2011. www.gallup.com/poll/154169/chronic-pain-rates-shoot-until-americans-reach-late-50s.aspx.

the training would tend to make doctors even more suspicious of patients seeking pain treatment.

Exaggerating the "Epidemic"

To justify a crackdown that will be effective only if it hurts people in pain, the Office of National Drug Control Policy says we are experiencing a "prescription drug abuse crisis" that amounts to an "epidemic." Although there is little evidence of such an epidemic in the federal government's own survey data, the number of fatal overdoses involving opioid analgesics nearly quadrupled between 1999 and 2007. Meanwhile, the amount of opioids prescribed per person has increased by an even larger percentage, meaning the risk of overdose is smaller today than it was a decade ago.

These overdose deaths mainly result from careless decisions by nonmedical users who either take too much or mix narcotic painkillers with other depressants. All the talk of an "epidemic," which brings to mind a deadly microbe that infects people who have no choice in the matter, tends to conceal this reality. *The New York Times* says OxyContin "hurtled through" an Ohio town, as if it were a tornado indiscriminately wreaking havoc instead of a drug deliberately taken by people who like its psychoactive effects.

By contrast, people who suffer from severe chronic pain as a result of car crashes, botched surgeries, or degenerative conditions do not choose to be in that situation. It's bad enough that they are forced to beg government-appointed gatekeepers for relief. They should not be punished further because of other people's reckless choices.

TWELVE

A Teenage Girl Describes Her Experience with Heroin Addiction

Anonymous, as told to Jane Bianchi

> In the following viewpoint, originally told to Jane Bianchi, senior news editor of *Seventeen* magazine, an anonymous teenage girl shares the story of her struggle with heroin addiction. She started using heroin when a new boyfriend introduced her to the drug, and soon she and her two best friends were using it every day. She was finally able to kick her heroin addiction, but her two friends overdosed and died.

I'll always remember driving around my Michigan suburb with Briona and Erika, my two BFFs. We'd blast [singer] Sara Evans's "A Little Bit Stronger" and sing at the top of our lungs. Then we'd go to the mall to try on the most expensive clothes and take funny pictures of ourselves. Those were our favorite things to do—besides heroin.

Bad Habits Developed in a Group

I met Bri during sophomore year of high school. At the time, I was a B student and an all-league crosscountry runner. We became

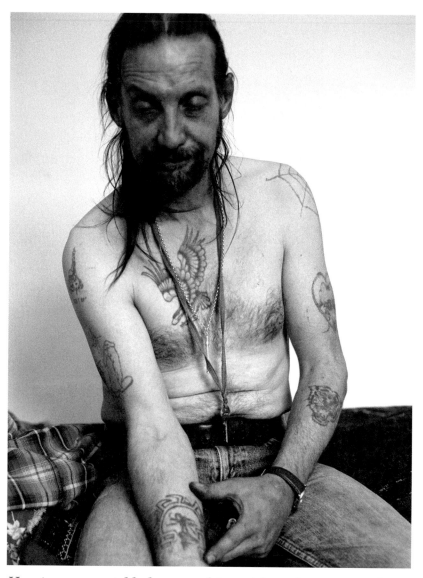

Heroin users quickly become thin, with sunken eyes and pale skin.

close when we started dating guys who were best friends. Her boyfriend and mine were the coolest, most powerful guys at school. We knew they were drug dealers and thought that made them bad-a **. They got us into the best parties and bought us jewelry. They made us feel popular!

After a few months of dating, my boyfriend offered me heroin at his house. Like a lot of kids at school, I had smoked pot and taken prescription painkillers on occasion, but heroin seemed scarier. Still, I was afraid that if I said no, my boyfriend would leave me and find another girl who'd say yes. I trusted him and figured that he'd never do anything to hurt me.

Heroin made me feel numb to my problems. It made me stop worrying about getting good grades or running faster. While I was getting hooked, Bri's boyfriend was introducing her to heroin at his house. And when Erika, a cute hippie girl in my math class, and I became friendly, I told her that I had tried heroin. She asked if she could try some too. Within months, she, Bri and I were getting high together every day—before school in the car, in the bathroom at lunch, and then after school at the guys' houses. It became a fun, secret escape that bonded us together. When we were high, nothing bothered us—we felt free.

But when you're on heroin for a while, you look like a zombie. I lost color in my skin, my eyes became sunken in, and I was emaciated. It's so hard to stop, because it's so addictive. If I didn't find a way to get high, I'd go through withdrawal—the worst sickness I've ever experienced. I'd get the chills, the shakes, and nausea until I shot up again to make those feelings go away. That's when I'd truly feel gross, like an addict.

Our habits got so bad that we'd each spend $140 a day to stay high and avoid withdrawal. We did grimy things to get money. We'd steal jewelry from friends' houses and pawn it. One time I stole $3,000 from my twin sister's college savings fund! As punishment, my parents kicked me out of the house for a little while. I am deeply ashamed now, but back then, I didn't care. My only focus was getting more drugs.

By junior year, my life had fallen apart. I quit running, I lost any friends who didn't do drugs, and my family was fed up with me. I got kicked out of school for skipping class, and then I got kicked out of an alternative school for drug possession. Next I got kicked out of rehab for breaking rules and went to jail for six months. When I was lying on a concrete bench in jail using a toilet paper roll for a pillow, I felt like a criminal. During that time, Erika was

How the Route of Use Affects the Speed and Intensity of a Drug's Effect

The method by which a drug is consumed determines how quickly it will take effect and how long it will last (shown here as "concentration in the brain"). Generally speaking, drugs that take effect quickly and wear off quickly tend to be more addictive—for example, injecting (or "shooting up") heroin is extremely addictive. Injecting drugs also carries a high risk of overdose and has other adverse health consequences.

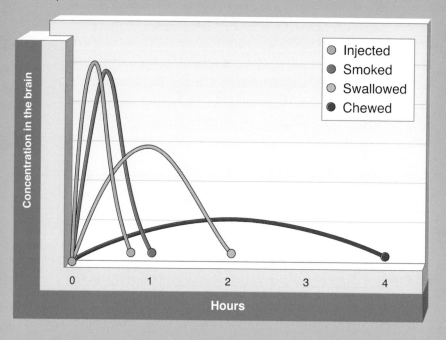

Taken from: David Nutt. *Drugs Without the Hot Air: Minimizing the Harms of Legal and Illegal Drugs.* Cambridge: UIT Cambridge Ltd., 2012, p. 178.

also in and out of jail, and Bri did some time in a juvenile detention center. We had no choice but to get clean. The withdrawal was horrible, but it was a relief to wake up and not need heroin.

But the moment we all got out, we fell right back into our old habit of getting high together. We had no idea how to be around each other and not do drugs. About once a month, one of us would overdose and get rushed to the hospital. Doctors always brought us back, though. We felt so invincible that even before we'd leave the hospital parking lot, we'd do heroin again.

Last February [2011], I went into withdrawal and decided to quit—and I wanted to convince Bri and Erika to quit, too. But then I got a call from Erika. "Bri died! She overdosed last night!" she said, hysterical. I didn't believe her at first. I kept calling Bri's phone over and over, just to hear her voice on the message. Slowly it sunk in. She wasn't going to answer the phone. Erika and I hung out two nights later, and she said, "Do you want to use just one more time?" I said, "Absolutely not." And she shrugged and said, "One more time won't kill me."

But she was wrong. Just when I thought life couldn't get any worse, Erika died from an apparent heroin overdose, too. After I had gone home that night, she used in her bedroom.

Learning from Loss

It's been months, and I'm still figuring out how to live without my BFFs. At first, I thought it was a crazy coincidence. But now I think: No, this is what happens when you do heroin. People die.

I broke up with my boyfriend, and I haven't touched drugs since. I'm not clean because rehab or jail forced me into it. I'm clean because I want to be.

I've been volunteering to tell my story at high schools, drug courts, and juvenile detention centers in my county. I want teens to know that this drug doesn't care how old you are or what you have going for you—it just wants to kill you. I somehow survived, so I want to tell Bri and Erika's story to make sure they didn't die for no reason.

What You Should Know About Drug Abuse

Facts About Drug Abuse

The Centers for Disease Control and Prevention (CDC) reported on June 8, 2012, that of students nationwide

- 44.7 percent had ever tried cigarette smoking;
- 18.1 percent currently smoke cigarettes;
- in 1991 81.6 percent had ever drunk alcohol, declining to 70.8 percent in 2011;
- current alcohol use was 50.8 percent in 1991, declining to 38.7 percent in 2011;
- the prevalence of binge drinking was 31.3 percent in 1991; in 2011 it was 21.9 percent;
- 31.3 percent had ever used marijuana in 1991, increasing to 39.9 percent in 2011;
- 14.7 percent were current marijuana users in 1991, rising to 23.1 percent in 2011;
- 3 percent were current users of cocaine;
- 11.4 percent had used inhalants;
- in 2001, 11.1 percent had ever used ecstasy; in 2011, 8.2 percent had done so;
- 2.9 percent had ever used heroin;
- in 1999, 9.1 percent had ever used methamphetamine, declining to 3.8 percent in 2011;
- in 2001, 13.3 percent had ever used hallucinogens, dropping to 8.7 percent in 2011;

- 20.7 percent had ever taken prescription drugs without a doctor's prescription.

According to the *2011 National Survey on Drug Use and Health: Summary of National Findings* published by the US Department of Health and Human Services (HHS),

- an estimated 22.5 million Americans aged twelve or older were current (in the past month) illicit drug users;
- marijuana was the most commonly used illicit drug, with 18.1 million past-month users;
- there were 1.4 million current cocaine users;
- 439,000 people had used methamphetamine in the past month;
- 620,000 people had used heroin in the past year;
- 972,000 persons had used hallucinogens by in the past month;
- 6.1 million persons (2.4 percent) had used prescription psychotherapeutic drugs nonmedically in the past month;
- among unemployed adults aged eighteen or older in 2011, 17.2 percent were current illicit drug users, which was higher than the 8 percent of those employed full-time and 11.6 percent of those employed part-time;
- there were an estimated 133.4 million current drinkers of alcohol in 2011;
- there were approximately 9.7 million underage drinkers in 2011, including 6.1 million binge drinkers and 1.7 million heavy drinkers;
- an estimated 68.2 million Americans aged twelve or older were current (in the past month) users of a tobacco product;
- an estimated 20.6 million persons (8.0 percent of the population aged twelve or older) were classified as being substance dependent or substance abusers in the past year (of these, 2.6 million were classified as dependent on or abusers of both alcohol and illicit drugs, 3.9 million had dependence on or abused illicit drugs but not alcohol, and 14.1 million had dependence on or abused alcohol but not illicit drugs);

- the number of persons with marijuana dependence or abuse did not change between 2002 and 2011, remaining at 4.2 million;
- between 2004 and 2011, the number of people with pain reliever dependence or abuse increased from 1.4 million to 1.8 million;
- between 2006 and 2011, the number with cocaine dependence or abuse declined from 1.7 million to 0.8 million;
- the number of persons with heroin dependence or abuse increased from 214,000 in 2007 to 426,000 in 2011; and
- between 2002 and 2011, the percentage of youths aged twelve to seventeen with substance dependence or abuse declined from 8.9 percent to 6.9 percent.

The United Nations Office on Drugs and Crime *World Drug Report 2012*, reported that

- about 12 percent of users of illegal drugs are "problem drug users";
- of the earth's 7 billion people, an estimated 230 million people take an illegal drug on at least one occasion each year, or approximately 1 in 20 people aged 15–64;
- about 1 in 40 people take illegal drugs at least once per month;
- about one of every 160 people, or 27 million people around the world, use illegal drugs in a way that presents significant health risks;
- illegal drug use is primarily associated with young users in most areas of the world, with use rates gradually increasing throughout the teen years, peaking at ages 18–25, and slowly declining to low levels among those aged 65 or older;
- the US rate of illicit drug use peaks at about age 18–20; for alcohol and tobacco, peak use rates happen between ages 20 and 25;
- in the United States, illicit drug use takes place among 7.9 percent of the population aged 12 or older in rural areas, compared with 16.2 percent in large cities;

- US households that earned less than $20,000 in 2010 had a rate of illicit drug use of 21 percent while among those with household incomes over $75,000, the rate was 12.4 percent.

Costs and Consequences of Drug Abuse

According to the HHS's *2011 National Survey on Drug Use and Health: Summary of National Findings*,

- 9.4 million persons aged 12 or older (3.7 percent) reported driving under the influence of illicit drugs during the past year (the rate was highest among young adults aged 18 to 25 [11.6 percent]);
- adults aged 21 or older who had first used alcohol at age 14 or younger were more than seven times as likely to be classified as alcohol dependent or abusers than adults who had their first drink at age 21 or older (13.8 vs. 1.8 percent).

The Drug Abuse Warning Network reported on December 28, 2010, that

- in 2009, there were nearly 4.6 million drug-related emergency department (ED) visits, of which about one-half (49.8 percent, or 2.3 million) were attributed to adverse reactions to pharmaceuticals and almost one-half (45.1 percent, or 2.1 million) were attributed to drug misuse or abuse;
- of the 2.1 million ED visits involving drug misuse or abuse in 2009, 1.2 million visits involved the misuse or abuse of pharmaceuticals, almost 1 million were related to illicit drugs, and about 200,000 visits were associated with underage drinking;
- alcohol was involved in more than 650,000 ED visits;
- patients aged twenty or younger accounted for 19.1 percent (877,802 visits) of all drug-related ED visits in 2009, and about one-half (415,351) of these visits involved drug misuse or abuse;
- for ED visits related to the use of illicit drugs, cocaine and marijuana had the highest rates of involvement at 137.7 and 122.6 visits per 100,000 population, respectively;

- ED visits involving alcohol in combination with other drugs occurred at a rate of 169.3 visits per 100,000 population;
- ED visits involving ecstasy increased by 123.2 percent from 2004 to 2009;
- for patients aged twenty or younger, ED visits resulting from misuse or abuse of pharmaceuticals increased 45.4 percent between 2004 and 2009 (116,644 and 169,589 visits, respectively).

The United Nations Office on Drugs and Crime *World Drug Report 2012*, reported that

- around the world in 2010, an estimated 99,000–253,000 deaths occurred due to use of illicit drugs in the fifteen to sixty-four age group (0.5–1.3 percent of all deaths in that age group);
- in North America 44,800 deaths due to use of illicit drugs were reported in 2010;
- poisoning is the leading cause of death due to injuries; about nine-tenths of deaths from poisoning are due to drug use;
- 12 percent of those who use illicit drugs become dependent on the drug, but this rate varies depending on the drug involved:
- over 50 percent of heroin users develop dependency;
- 26 percent of methamphetamine users develop dependency;
- 15 percent of cocaine users develop dependency; and
- 10 percent of marijuana users develop dependency.

The National Drug Intelligence Center (NDIC) *2011 National Drug Threat Assessment* reports that

- in 2007 illicit drug use cost society over $193 billion, of which
    - crime-related costs amounted to an estimated $61.4 billion,
    - health-related costs were an estimated $11.4 billion, and
    - lost productivity accounted for an estimated $120.3 billion;

- car accidents involving use of legal or illegal drugs in which the driver was killed increased from 3,710 in 2005 to 3,952 in 2009;
- the overall number of people killed in such accidents was 37,646 in 2005 and 28,936 in 2009;
- in 2009, there were 171 fires or explosions at locations where methamphetamine was being produced.

According to *War on Drugs: Report of the Global Commission on Drug Policy*, published in June 2011,

- deaths in Mexico related to the illegal drug trade are estimated to exceed 50,000 since the government there began cracking down on drug cartels in 2006;
- an additional 10,000 people are estimated to be missing since 2006 as a result of drug-related violence in Mexico;
- over 1.5 million people in Mexico are estimated to have been displaced since 2006 due to the drug violence in that country.

According to the National Center on Addiction and Substance Abuse at Columbia University (CASA), in its June 2011 report *Adolescent Substance Use: America's #1 Public Health Problem*,

- 1.6 million high school students (11.9 percent) could be diagnosed as having a substance use disorder as a result of alcohol, nicotine, or other drug use;
- of those who started using alcohol, nicotine, or other drugs before turning eighteen, one in four are addicted, and in comparison, of those who started using when they were twenty-one or older, only one in twenty-five are addicted;
- underage drinking incurs financial costs of an estimated $68 billion each year;
- juvenile justice programs related to drug abuse cost an estimated $14.4 billion each year;
- total costs from factors such as crime, disease, child abuse and neglect, accidents, accidental pregnancies, and homelessness at the local, state, and federal levels related to drug

use in the entire US population amount to an estimated $467.7 billion annually, or $1,500 for each person in the United States;

- adolescents who use alcohol, tobacco, or marijuana have twice the risk of having poor grades as those who do not use those drugs;
- about 20 percent of young adults and teens report having unprotected sex following use of alcohol or other drugs;
- 33.9 million children aged seventeen or younger (45.4 percent) live with a parent who uses drugs in a risky manner;
- over 12.6 million children aged seventeen or younger (16.9 percent) live with a parent who has a substance abuse disorder.

According to the US Senate Caucus on International Narcotics Control's June 2012 report *Reducing the U.S. Demand for Illegal Drugs*,

- 36,450 people in the United States died as a result of unintentional drug overdose in 2008, and of these, 20,044, or 55 percent, were the result of prescription painkiller use;
- in 2009 there were fourteen calls to US poison control centers concerning synthetic marijuana, while in 2010 there were 2,882 such calls and in 2011 there were 6,348 such calls;
- in 2010 there were 303 calls to US poison control centers concerning drugs called "bath salts," while in 2011 there were 5,853 such calls.

Availability of Drugs to Youth
According to the *2011 National Survey on Drug Use and Health: Summary of National Findings*, published by HHS,

- 47.7 percent of youths aged twelve to seventeen reported that it would be "fairly easy" or "very easy" for them to obtain marijuana;
- 17.5 percent reported it would be easy to get cocaine;
- 12.2 percent indicated that LSD would be easily available;
- 10.7 percent reported easy availability for heroin;

- in 2010–2011, among persons aged twelve or older who used pain relievers nonmedically in the past twelve months, 54.2 percent got the drug they most recently used from a friend or relative for free, 18.1 percent reported they got the drug from a doctor, 3.9 percent got pain relievers from a drug dealer or other stranger, and 0.3 percent bought them on the Internet.

CASA's *National Survey of American Attitudes on Substance Abuse XVII: Teens*, published in August 2012, reports that

- according to 52 percent of high school students surveyed, there is a location on or near school grounds where students go during school hours to use drugs (including alcohol and tobacco);
- 36 percent of high school students report that it is not difficult for students to get away with using tobacco, alcohol, or other drugs during school hours;
- 44 percent of high school students say they know a drug dealer at their school;
- 32 percent of students in middle school and 60 percent of those in high school report that students sell, use, or keep drugs on the school grounds.

Drug Abuse Prevention and Treatment

According to the *2011 National Survey on Drug Use and Health: Summary of National Findings*, published by HHS,

- 75.1 percent of youths aged twelve to seventeen reported having seen or heard drug or alcohol prevention messages from sources outside of school, while 74.6 percent heard such messages at school;
- 21.6 million people aged twelve or older (8.4 percent) needed treatment for an illicit drug or alcohol use problem, and of these, 2.3 million (10.6 percent of those who needed treatment) received treatment at a specialty facility, meaning that 19.3 million people (89.4 percent) of those who needed treatment for an illicit drug or alcohol use problem did not receive treatment at a specialty facility in the past

year; and of the 19.3 million persons classified as needing substance use treatment who did not receive treatment, 912,000 persons (4.7 percent) reported that they felt they needed treatment for their illicit drug or alcohol use problem; and of these 912,000 persons who felt they needed treatment, 281,000 (30.8 percent) reported that they made an effort to get treatment, while 631,000 (69.2 percent) reported making no effort to get treatment.

The National Institute on Drug Abuse (NIDA) reported in March 2011 that

- In 2008, of 1.8 million people who were admitted for treatment of drug abuse,
    - 41.4 percent were admitted for alcohol (in 18.3 percent of cases another drug was also involved);
    - 17 percent were admitted for marijuana;
    - 14.1 percent were admitted for heroin;
    - 8.1 percent were admitted for crack (smokable cocaine);
    - 6.5 percent were admitted for stimulants;
    - 5.9 percent were admitted for opiates (other than heroin);
    - 3.2 percent were admitted for nonsmoked cocaine;
    - 0.6 percent were admitted for tranquilizers ;
    - 0.2 percent were admitted for PCP;
    - 0.2 percent were admitted for sedatives;
    - 0.1 percent were admitted for hallucinogens;
    - 0.1 percent were admitted for inhalants;
    - 0.4 percent were admitted for other drugs; and
    - in 2.2 percent of cases no specific drug was reported.

According to CASA's June 2011 report *Adolescent Substance Use: America's #1 Public Health Problem,*

- of the estimated 1.6 million high school students who have a diagnosable substance use disorder, only 99,913 (6.4 percent) have had drug abuse treatment in the previous year;

- only 28 percent of drug abuse treatment facilities in the United States have programs specifically designed for adolescents;
- of adolescents getting treatment for drug abuse,
  - the criminal justice system referred 48.2 percent for treatment;
  - schools referred 11.2 percent; and
  - health care professionals referred 4.7 percent.

According to CASA's *Addiction Medicine: Closing the Gap Between Science and Practice,* published in June 2012,

- approximately 70 percent of those with major depression, hypertension, or diabetes receive treatment for their health condition, while, in contrast, only about 10 percent of those addicted to alcohol, nicotine, or other drugs receive treatment for their addiction;
- in 2008 only 42.1 percent of those admitted for addiction treatment completed their treatment;
- 14.8 percent of those admitted for treatment received short-term residential treatment, which had a completion rate of 54.8 percent;
- longer-term residential treatment accounted for 11.4 percent of all admissions and had a completion rate of 45.5 percent;
- nonresidential treatment services accounted for the majority of admissions (73.8 percent) but had a completion rate of only 39.1 percent.

Public Opinion on Drug Abuse

An Angus Reid Public Opinion poll published on July 21, 2010, found that

- 64 percent of respondents believe that "America has a serious drug abuse problem and it affects the whole country";
- 20 percent of respondents believe only specific areas and people have a problem with drug abuse;
- 7 percent of respondents do not believe that America has a drug abuse problem;

- 8 percent of those polled believe the war on drugs is a success;
- 65 percent believe it is a failure;
- 27 percent were not sure if it has succeeded or failed;
- 52 percent of those polled support the legalization of marijuana;
- 10 percent support legalization of ecstasy;
- legalization of powder cocaine, crystal meth, and heroin was supported by 8 percent each;
- 7 percent support legalizing crack cocaine.

According to CASA's June 2011 report *Adolescent Substance Use: America's #1 Public Health Problem*,

- only 42.6 percent of parents indicated the following as a top-three concern for their teenagers: alcohol, cigarettes, prescription drugs used for nonmedical purposes, or illegal drugs.
- 20.8 percent of parents believe marijuana is a harmless drug.

What You Should Do About Drug Abuse

Gather Information

The first step in grappling with any complex and controversial issue is to be informed about it. Gather as much information as you can from a variety of sources. The essays in this book form an excellent starting point as they represent a variety of viewpoints and approaches to the topic. Your school or local public library will be another source of useful information; look there for relevant books, magazines, and encyclopedia entries. The bibliography and organizations to contact section of this book will give you useful starting points in gathering additional information.

There is a wealth of information and perspectives on drug abuse in both the US and international media. Internet search engines will be helpful to you in your research. Many blogs and websites have information and articles dealing with the topic from a variety of perspectives, including concerned individuals offering their opinions; activist organizations; governmental organizations such as the National Institute on Drug Abuse; and popular media outlets.

A wealth of articles, books, and other resources that deal with the topic have been published in recent years; as well, many academic papers on drug abuse are available online. If the information in such papers is too dense or technical, check the abstract at the beginning of the article, which provides a clear summary of the researcher's conclusions.

You may also want to find and interview people who have experienced drug abuse firsthand or who have worked with addicts. Most areas have organizations that help those with drug abuse issues, such as Narcotics Anonymous. Such groups can be contacted by phone or via the Internet (start with the organizations to contact section of this book).

Identify the Issues

Once you have gathered your information, review it methodically to discover the key issues involved. Why do people use or abuse drugs? What (if anything) distinguishes drug *use* from drug *abuse*? Are some drugs, or methods of ingestion, more dangerous than others? What is known about the causes of drug abuse and addiction and how best to treat those conditions? How can the many harms associated with drug abuse be reduced? Is it possible to completely eliminate nonmedical use of drugs and, if so, would that be a desirable goal for society? How has drug prohibition, or the war on drugs, affected patterns of drug use and the risks associated with the use and abuse of drugs? What distinguishes legal drugs of abuse, such as alcohol and tobacco, from illegal drugs of abuse, such as marijuana or cocaine? It may be worthwhile to consider how drug use and abuse have shown up—and been dealt with—in other cultures and time periods, to get a broader perspective on what is happening in America today.

You may find that approaches to dealing with drug abuse vary, depending on the beliefs of the people or agencies involved. For example, those who consider drug abuse primarily as a brain disease may emphasize approaches that work directly or indirectly with brain processes. Others may stress social factors such as growing up in a disadvantaged or abusive environment and work to change those conditions. Or a more holistic or integral approach may be taken that attempts to address many different aspects of the problem at the same time.

Evaluate Your Information Sources

In developing your own opinion, it is vital to evaluate the sources of the information you have discovered. Authors of books and magazine articles, etc., however well-intentioned, have their own perspectives and biases that may affect how they present information on the subject. Drug abuse is a controversial and complicated issue, and people have very different ways of looking at it. In some cases people and organizations may deliberately distort information to support a strongly held ideological or moral position—signs of this include oversimplification and extreme positions.

Consider the authors' credentials and what organizations they are affiliated with. For example, someone from the US Drug Enforcement Administration may emphasize legal and military approaches aimed at eliminating the supply of prohibited drugs. Someone who works with drug addicts may emphasize harm reduction approaches designed to make drug use less dangerous. On the other hand, if you find someone arguing against their expected bias—for example, a police officer arguing in favor of drug legalization—it may be worthwhile to pay particular attention to what he or she is saying. Always critically evaluate and assess your sources rather than take whatever they say as factual.

Examine Your Own Perspective

Drug abuse is a complex and emotionally charged topic. Spend some time exploring your own thoughts and feelings about it. Consider the attitudes and beliefs on this issue that you have received from family members, friends, and the media throughout your life. Such messages affect your own thoughts and feelings about the subject. Have you or anyone you know ever used, abused, or been addicted to drugs? If you or someone close to you has experienced significant difficulties or negative consequences as a result of drug abuse or addiction, that may make it more challenging for you to form a clear view of the issues involved, and/or it may give you special insight into the topic. Be wary of "confirmation bias," the tendency to seek out information that confirms what one already believes to be true, and to discount information that contradicts one's preexisting beliefs. Deliberately counter this tendency by seeking out perspectives that contradict your current beliefs and asking yourself whether they might be true.

Form Your Own Opinion and Take Action

Once you have gathered and organized information, identified the issues involved, and examined your own perspective, you will be ready to form an opinion on drug abuse and to advocate your position in debates and discussions (and if you or someone close to you is having difficulties with drugs, you will have a better idea of what resources and approaches are available to deal with the problem). Perhaps you will conclude that one of the viewpoints you have encountered offers the best explanation of what causes drug abuse and how to deal with it, or you may decide that a number of approaches working together are needed to adequately address this complex issue. You might even decide that none of the perspectives on drug abuse that you have encountered are convincing to you and that you cannot take a decisive position as yet. If that is the case, ask yourself what you would need to know to make up your mind; perhaps a bit more research would be helpful. Whatever position you take, be prepared to explain it clearly based on facts, evidence, and well-thought-out beliefs.

ORGANIZATIONS TO CONTACT

The editors have compiled the following list of organizations concerned with the issues debated in this book. The descriptions are
derived from materials provided by the organizations. All have
publications or information available for interested readers. The
list was compiled on the date of publication of the present volume; names, addresses, phone and fax numbers, and e-mail and
Internet addresses may change. Be aware that many organizations
take several weeks or longer to respond to inquiries, so allow as
much time as possible.

Drug Free America Foundation
5999 Central Ave., Ste. 301
Saint Petersburg, FL 33710
(727) 828-0211
fax: (727) 828-0212
website: www.dfaf.org

Drug Free America Foundation is a nongovernmental drug prevention and policy organization committed to developing, pro-
moting, and sustaining global strategies, policies, and laws that
will reduce illegal drug use, drug addiction, and drug-related
injuries and deaths. Its reference collection contains more than
twenty-one hundred books and other media chronicling the rise
of the drug culture and current drug policy issues. It favors the
war on drugs, and its website contains many articles defending
current policy, including student drug testing.

Erowid
PO Box 1116
Grass Valley, CA 95945
e-mail: sage@erowid.org
website: www.erowid.org

Erowid is a member-supported organization whose mission is to provide access to reliable information about psychoactive plants, chemicals, and related issues. It works with academic, medical, and experiential experts to develop and publish new resources, as well as to improve and increase access to already existing resources. The organization's website provides information on hundreds of psychoactive substances, including effects, legal status, and health considerations. Of particular note are the Experience Vaults, which contain close to a hundred thousand firsthand descriptions of psychoactive drug use. Erowid also provides links to online books about psychoactive drugs and publishes the newsletter *Erowid Extracts* twice a year.

Independent Scientific Committee on Drugs (ISCD)
Centre for Crime and Justice Studies
2 Langley Lane
London SW8 1GB
United Kingdom
e-mail: info@drugscience.org.uk
website: www.drugscience.org.uk

The ISCD is the leading independent scientific body in the United Kingdom on the harms and benefits of both legal and controlled drugs. Its drug scientists work together to ensure that the public can access clear, evidence-based information on drugs without interference from political or commercial interests. The organization addresses issues surrounding drug harms and benefits; regulation and education; and prevention, treatment, and recovery. Its website offers detailed information on numerous drugs (both legal and illegal), a newsletter, links to additional resources on the Internet, and links to follow David Nutt (the chairman of the organization) on Facebook and Twitter.

Integral Recovery
PO Box 146
Teasdale, UT 84773
(435) 691-1193
e-mail: johndupuy@gmail.com
website: www.integralrecovery.com

Integral Recovery is an addiction recovery program founded by John Dupuy that attempts to address all relevant aspects of body, mind, heart, and spirit to achieve recovery from substance addiction and enhanced health and well-being. Its website offers articles, audio, and video material on addiction recovery, as well as a blog by John Dupuy. Consultation and coaching services are available, as well as recommendations for other programs to help addicts and their families.

International Centre for Science in Drug Policy (ICSDP)
608–1081 Burrard St.
Vancouver, BC V6Z 1Y6
Canada
e-mail: info@icsdp.org
website: www.icsdp.org

The ICSDP is an international network of scientists, academics, and health practitioners committed to improving the health and safety of communities and individuals affected by illicit drugs. The network includes leading experts from around the world who have come together in an effort to inform illicit drug policies with the best available scientific evidence. The organization's website offers research reports and summaries, a blog, press releases, an e-mail newsletter and e-alerts, as well as links to follow the ICSDP's work through Facebook and Twitter.

Law Enforcement Against Prohibition (LEAP)
121 Mystic Ave., Stes. 7–9
Medford, MA 02155
(781) 393-6985
fax: (781) 393-2964
e-mail: info@leap.cc
website: www.leap.cc

LEAP is a nonprofit educational organization founded by police officers. Its mission is to reduce the multitude of unintended harmful consequences resulting from fighting the war on drugs. Its website contains many articles and multimedia presentations explaining why it believes legalizing drugs would be a more effective way of reducing the crime, disease, and addiction that drugs cause. Publications offered on the LEAP website include *End Prohibition Now!*, *Why I Want All Drugs Legalized*, and *Ending the Drug War: A Dream Deferred (2011)*. Other offerings include videos, a blog, the *LEAP Newsletter*, and links to LEAP feeds on Facebook, Twitter, YouTube, and Myspace.

Multidisciplinary Association for Psychedelic Studies (MAPS)
309 Cedar St. #2323
Santa Cruz, CA 95060
(831) 429-6362
fax: (831) 429-6370
e-mail: askmaps@maps.org
website: http://maps.org

MAPS is a nonprofit research and educational organization that aims to educate the public about the risks and benefits of psychedelics and marijuana and to develop those substances into prescription medicines. Its website offers a vast array of information, including reports on medical marijuana and the use of psychedelics such as ibogaine and ayahuasca to treat drug addiction, research papers, free literature, and audio and video material. An e-mail newsletter is available, as well as the triannual publication *MAPS Bulletin*, the entire archives of which are available on the website. MAPS also hosts a moderated discussion forum via e-mail.

Narcotics Anonymous
PO Box 9999
Van Nuys, CA 91409
(818) 773-9999
fax: (818) 700-0700
e-mail: fsmail@na.org
website: www.na.org

Established in the 1950s, Narcotics Anonymous supports more than twenty thousand groups in America and some one hundred foreign countries, which hold more than thirty thousand weekly meetings a year. The meetings serve as forums for members to help one another emerge from their addictions. The vision of Narcotics Anonymous is for every addict in the world to have the chance to experience the organization's message in his or her own language and culture and find the opportunity for a new way of life. Its website offers the *Just for Today* daily meditation e-mail, NA World Services News, and a variety of literature on addiction recovery.

National Center on Addiction and Substance Abuse at Columbia University (CASA)
633 Third Ave., 19th Fl., New York, NY 10017-6706
(212) 841-5200
website: www.casacolumbia.org

CASA Columbia is a private nonprofit organization that works to educate the public about the hazards of chemical dependency. The organization supports treatment as the best way to reduce chemical dependency and produces numerous publications describing the harmful effects of alcohol and drug addiction and effective ways to address the problem of substance abuse. Books published by CASA Columbia include *High Society: How Substance Abuse Ravages America and What to Do About It* and *How to Raise a Drug-Free Kid: The Straight Dope for Parents*. Publications available on its website include *Addiction: A Preventable and Treatable Disease*, *National Survey of American Attitudes on Substance Abuse XVII: Teens*, and *Under the Counter: The Diversion and Abuse of Controlled Prescription Drugs in the U.S.* Its website also features videos and the quarterly *CASA Inside* newsletter.

National Institute on Drug Abuse (NIDA)
Office of Science Policy and Communications, Public Information and Liaison Branch
6001 Executive Blvd., Room 5213, MSC 9561
Bethesda, MD 20892-9561
(301) 443-1124

e-mail: information@nida.nih.gov
website: www.drugabuse.gov

NIDA is one of the National Institutes of Health, a component of the US Department of Health and Human Services. NIDA supports and conducts research on drug abuse to improve addiction prevention, treatment, and policy efforts. It is dedicated to understanding how drugs of abuse affect the brain and behavior, and it works to rapidly disseminate new information to policy makers, drug abuse counselors, and the general public. It publishes the *NIDA Notes* and *What's New at NIDA?* newsletters; "DrugFacts" summarizing key information on many different mind-altering substances; and a variety of more-detailed publications, including *Seeking Drug Abuse Treatment: Know What to Ask, Drugs: Shatter the Myths*, and *Marijuana: Facts for Teens*. The website also offers videos, podcasts, e-books, and a section on related topics such as addiction science, drug testing, prevention research, and trends and statistics. Of particular note is the "NIDA for teens" section at http://teens.drugabuse.gov.

Office of National Drug Control Policy (ONDCP)
Drug Policy Information Clearinghouse, PO Box 6000
Rockville, MD 20849-6000
(800) 666-3332
fax: (301) 519-5212
e-mail: ondcp@ncjrs.org
website: www.whitehouse.gov/ondcp

The ONDCP is responsible for formulating the government's national drug strategy and the president's antidrug policy, as well as coordinating the federal agencies responsible for stopping drug trafficking. It has launched drug prevention programs, including the National Youth Antidrug Media Campaign and Above the Influence. ONDCP publications include *Price and Purity of Illicit Drugs: 1981–2007* and *Epidemic: Responding to America's Prescription Drug Abuse Crisis*. The ONDCP's website features fact sheets titled *Synthetic Drugs, Alternatives to Incarceration*, and *A Medical Approach to Drug Prevention*, as well as a blog, news releases, and information on treatment and recovery.

The Partnership at Drugfree.org
405 Lexington Ave., Ste. 1601
New York, NY 10174
(212) 922-1560
website: www.drugfree.org

The Partnership at Drugfree.org, previously known as the Partnership for a Drug-Free America, is a nonprofit organization that utilizes the media to reduce demand for illicit drugs in America. Best known for its national antidrug advertising campaign, the partnership works to educate children about the dangers of drugs and to prevent drug use among youth. It produces the *Partnership Newsletter*, annual reports, and monthly press releases about current events with which the partnership is involved. Its website offers research reports such as *Full Report: Hispanic Teens Are Abusing Drugs/Alcohol at Alarmingly Higher Levels* and *Survey Findings: More than Half of Massachusetts Parents Say Their Kids Have Access to Abusable Prescription Drugs in Their Homes*. Also available at its website are a drug guide to forty commonly abused drugs (available in both English and Spanish) and sections on prevention, intervention, treatment, and recovery.

US Drug Enforcement Administration (DEA)
Attn: Office of Diversion Control
8701 Morrissette Dr.
Springfield, VA 22152
(202) 307-1000
website: www.justice.gov/dea

The DEA is the federal agency charged with enforcing the nation's drug laws and regulations. It coordinates the activities of federal, state, and local agencies and works with foreign governments to reduce the availability of illicit drugs in the United States. The DEA publishes the biannual *Microgram Journal* and the monthly *Microgram Bulletin*. Numerous DEA publications are available on its website, including *Prescription for Disaster: How Teens Abuse Medicine, Get It Straight—the Facts About Drugs Student Guide* (2011), and *Speaking Out Against Drug Legalization* (2010). Drug fact sheets, videos, and a section specifically for teens (www.just-thinktwice.com/) can also be found on its website.

US Substance Abuse and Mental Health
Services Administration (SAMHSA)
1 Choke Cherry Rd.
Rockville, MD 20857
(877) 726-4727
fax: (240) 221-4292
e-mail: samhsainfo@samhsa.hhs.gov
website: www.samhsa.gov

The mission of SAMHSA is to reduce the impact of substance abuse and mental illness on America's communities. It aims to help create communities where individuals, families, schools, faith-based organizations, and workplaces take action to promote emotional health and reduce the likelihood of mental illness, substance abuse, and suicide. Publications available on its website include *Results from the 2011 National Survey on Drug Use and Health (NSDUH)*, *Substance Use Disorders in People with Physical and Sensory Disabilities*, *Tips for Teens: The Truth About Tobacco*, and brochures on a number of common drugs of abuse.

BIBLIOGRAPHY

Books

Joan Axelrod-Contrada, *The Facts About Drugs and Society*. New York: Marshall Cavendish/Benchmark, 2008.

Joseph A. Califano, *High Society: How Substance Abuse Ravages America and What to Do About It*. New York: Public Affairs, 2007.

Sylvia Engdahl, ed., *Issues on Trial: The War On Drugs*. Detroit: Greenhaven, 2009.

Kim Etingoff, *Abusing Over-the-Counter Drugs: Illicit Uses for Everyday Drugs*. Philadelphia: Mason Crest, 2008.

Steve Fox, Paul Armentano, and Mason Tvert, *Marijuana Is Safer: So Why Are We Driving People to Drink?* White River Junction, VT: Chelsea Green, 2009.

Margaret J. Goldstein, *Legalizing Drugs: Crime Stopper or Social Risk?* Minneapolis: Twenty-First Century, 2010.

Ellen Hopkins and Leah Wilson, *Flirtin' with the Monster: Your Favorite Authors on Ellen Hopkins' Crank and Glass*. Dallas: Benbella, 2009.

Kyle Keegan and Howard Moss, *Chasing the High: A Firsthand Account of One Young Person's Experience with Substance Abuse*. New York: Oxford University Press, 2008.

Marc D. Lewis, *Memoirs of an Addicted Brain: A Neuroscientist Examines His Former Life on Drugs*. New York: Public Affairs, 2012.

Hal Marcovitz, *Drug Abuse*. Detroit: Lucent, 2008.

Noël Merino, ed., *Opposing Viewpoints: Gateway Drugs*. Detroit: Greenhaven, 2008.

David Nutt, *Drugs Without the Hot Air: Minimising the Harms of Legal and Illegal Drugs*. Cambridge: UIT Cambridge, 2012.

Winifred Rosen and Andrew T. Weil, *From Chocolate to Morphine: Everything You Need to Know About Mind-Altering Drugs*. New York: Mariner, 2004.

Nic Sheff, *Tweak: Growing Up on Methamphetamines*. New York: Atheneum, 2009.

Sheila Stewart, *Hallucinogens: Unreal Visions*. Philadelphia: Mason Crest, 2008.

Hannah Westberg, *Hannah: My True Story of Drugs, Cutting, and Mental Illness*. Deerfield Beach, FL: Health Communications, 2010.

Periodicals & Internet Sources

Elizabeth Bernstein, "New Addiction on Campus: Raiding the Medicine Cabinet," *Wall Street Journal*, March 25, 2008.

Laura Carlsen, "The Drug War's Invisible Victims," America's Program, January 30, 2012. www.cipamericas.org/archives/6297.

Jimmy Carter, "Call Off the Global Drug War," *New York Times*, June 16, 2011.

Cory Doctorow, "Top US Drug Cop Can't Tell the Difference Between Marijuana and Heroin," Boing Boing, June 23, 2012. http://boingboing.net/2012/06/23/top-us-drug-cop-cant-tell-th.html.

Inge Fryklund, "On Drugs and Democracy," Foreign Policy in Focus, August 6, 2012. www.fpif.org/articles/on_drugs_and_democracy.

Froma Hardop, "The War Against Battered and Confused Addicts," Nation of Change, June 26, 2012. www.nationofchange.org/war-against-battered-and-confused-addicts-1340724329.

Sam Harris, "Drugs and the Meaning of Life," *Sam Harris* (blog), July 5, 2011. www.samharris.org/blog/item/drugs-and-the-meaning-of-life/.

William Harryman, "Drugs in Sports," Integral Options Cafe, August 7, 2007. http://integral-options.blogspot.com/2007/08/drugs-in-sports.html.

Chris Hedges, "A World of Hillbilly Heroin: The Hollowing Out of America, Up Close and Personal," Common Dreams, August 21, 2012. www.commondreams.org/view/2012/08/21-3.

Paul Hiebert, "Vancouver's Supervised Drug Injection Center: How Does It Work?," The Awl, April 30, 2012. www.theawl.com/2012/04/vancouver-supervised-drug-injection-center.

Jerome Hunt, "Why the Gay and Transgender Population Experiences Higher Rates of Substance Use," Center for American Progress, March 9, 2012. www.americanprogress.org/issues/lgbt/report/2012/03/09/11228/why-the-gay-and-transgender-population-experiences-higher-rates-of-substance-use/.

Nick King, "Middle-American Methamphetamine," *American Conservative*, April 5, 2011.

Jenny Marder, "Bath Salts: The Drug That Never Lets Go," *PBS Newshour*, September 20, 2012. www.pbs.org/newshour/multimedia/bath-salts/.

Howard Markel, "The D.S.M. Gets Addiction Right," *New York Times*, June 5, 2012.

Sarah Max, "Sex, Drugs and Recovery," *Time*, August 13, 2012.

Trevon Milliard, "Teen Substance Abuse: Lots of Questions, No Easy Answers," *Las Vegas Review-Journal*, June 17, 2012.

NIDA for Teens, "Anabolic Steroids," March 2012. http://teens.drugabuse.gov/facts/facts_ster1.php.

David Nutt, "Is the Future of Drugs Safe and Non-Addictive?," *Guardian* (Manchester, UK), June 10, 2012. www.guardian.co.uk/science/shortcuts/2012/jun/10/the-future-of-drugs-safe.

David Nutt, "The Miami Face-Eating Case Should Not Stampede US into a 'Bath Salts' Ban," *Guardian* (Manchester, UK), May 31, 2012. www.guardian.co.uk/commentisfree/2012/may/31/miami-face-eating-case-bath-salts-ban.

Tony O'Neill, "The Truth Behind the Bath Salt 'Epidemic,'" The Fix, June 17, 2012. www.thefix.com/content/bath-salt-scare-10084?page=all.

Steve Peck, "The Toll of Turning a Blind Eye to Drug Use During Military Service," *Huffington Post*, September 4, 2012. www.huffingtonpost.com/steve-peck/veterans-ptsd-drug-abuse_b_1853890.html.

Stanton Peele, "There Will Never Be a (Useful) Addiction Vaccine," *Huffington Post*, October 11, 2011. www.huffingtonpost.com/stanton-peele/controversy-with-addiction-vaccine_b_993594.html.

Jack Shafer, "Back-to-School Pharm Party: *Time* Magazine, the *Washington Post*, and Others Resurrect This Ancient Urban Myth," *Slate*, September 8, 2010. www.slate.com/articles/news_and_politics/press_box/2010/09/backtoschool_pharm_party.html.

Jamie Sotonoff, "Siblings of Drug Addicts Face Unique Pain," *Arlington Heights (IL) Daily Herald*, July 13, 2012. www.dailyherald.com/article/20120713/news/707139931/.

Jacob Sullum, "How Psychiatrists Make Drugs More Addictive," Reason.com, May 14, 2012. http://reason.com/blog/2012/05/14/how-psychiatrists-make-drugs-more-addict.

Maia Szalavitz, "How Childhood Trauma Creates Life-Long Adult Addicts," The Fix, September 25, 2011. www.thefix.com/content/trauma-and-addiction9180.

Maia Szalavitz, "The Legacy of the CIA's Secret LSD Experiments on America," *Time* Healthland, March 23, 2012. http://healthland.time.com/2012/03/23/the-legacy-of-the-cias-secret-lsd-experiments-on-america/.

Eve Turow, "The High Lands: Exploring Drug Tourism Across Southeast Asia," *Atlantic*, March 7, 2012.

Jacques Von Lunen, "Teens Do the Talking on How to Curb Substance Abuse," *Vancouver (WA) Columbian*, February 24, 2012. www.columbian.com/news/2012/feb/24/to-feel-to-trust-to-talk-anti-drug-inspiration-loc/.

Stephen C. Webster, "Scientist: Pushing OxyContin Addicts to Heroin Reveals 'Utter Failure' of Drug War," The Raw Story, July 13, 2012. www.rawstory.com/rs/2012/07/13/scientist-pushing-oxycontin-addicts-to-heroin-reveals-utter-failure-of-drug-war/.

PICTURE CREDITS